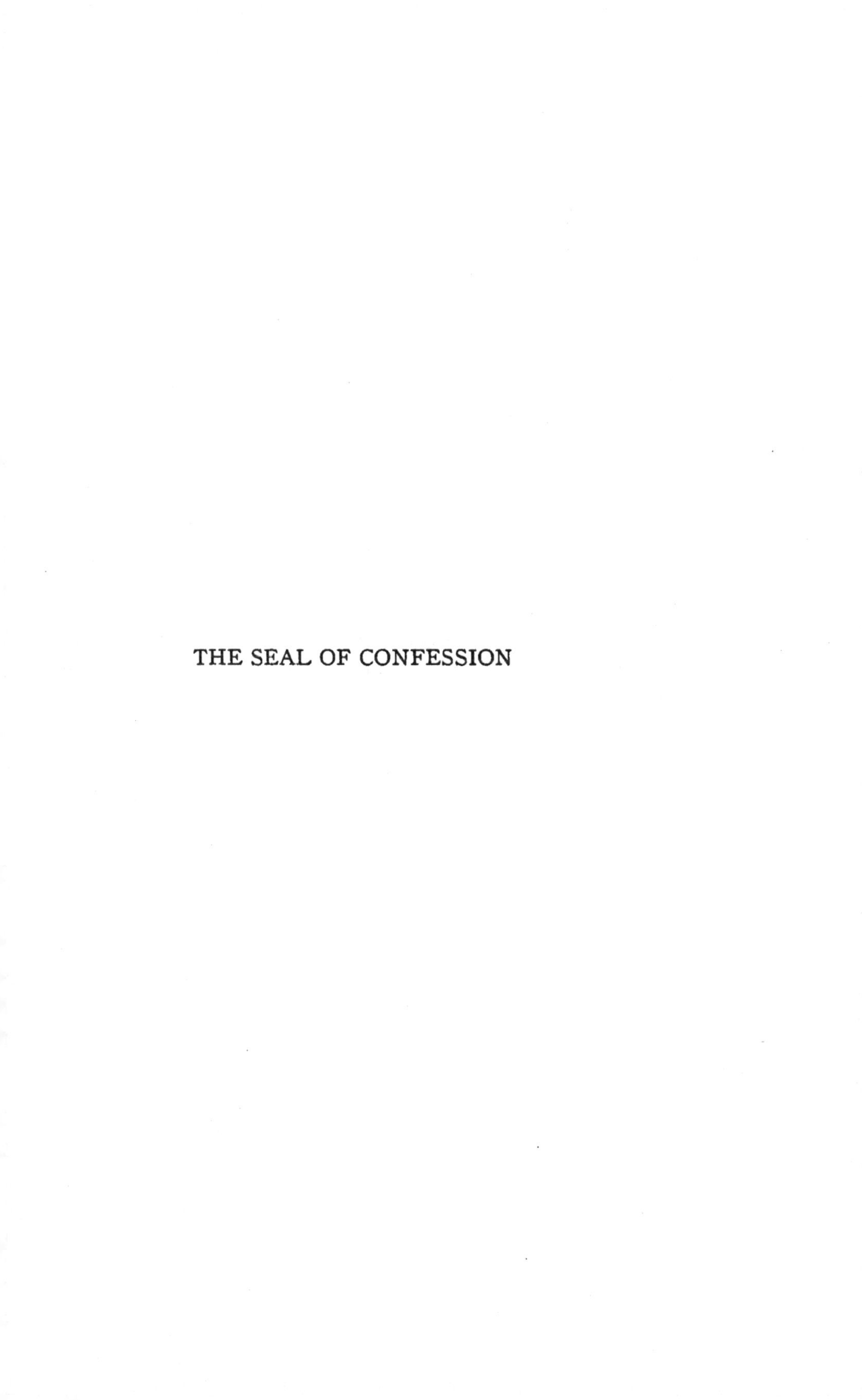

THE SEAL OF CONFESSION

This dissertation was approved by the Right Reverend Monsignor Clement V. Bastnagel, S.T.L., J.U.D., Associate Professor of Canon Law, as director and by the Reverend Romaeus O'Brien, O.Carm., J.C.D., and the Reverend Bernard F. Deutsch, J.C.D., I.C.D., as readers

THE CATHOLIC UNIVERSITY OF AMERICA
CANON LAW STUDIES
No. 413

The Seal of Confession

A DISSERTATION

SUBMITTED TO THE FACULTY OF THE SCHOOL OF CANON LAW OF THE CATHOLIC UNIVERSITY OF AMERICA IN PARTIAL FULFILLMENT OF THE REQUIREMENTS FOR THE DEGREE OF DOCTOR OF CANON LAW

BY

REVEREND JOHN R. ROOS, M.A., S.T.L., J.C.L.
PRIEST OF THE DIOCESE OF ALBANY

THE CATHOLIC UNIVERSITY OF AMERICA PRESS
WASHINGTON, D. C.
1960

NIHIL OBSTAT:

CLEMENT V. BASTNAGEL, S.T.L., J.U.D.
Censor Deputatus

Washington, D. C., May 31, 1960

IMPRIMATUR:

✠ WILLIAM A. SCULLY, D.D.
Bishop of Albany

Albany, N. Y., September 30, 1960

MURRAY AND HEISTER, INC.
WASHINGTON, D. C.

PRINTED BY
TIMES AND NEWS PUBLISHING CO.
GETTYSBURG, PA., U. S. A.

TO MY MOTHER AND FATHER

FOREWORD

It is a source of confidence for penitents, a tribute to the priesthood, and a cause for gratitude to God, that, in the words of the Holy Office, "the natural and divine law of the sacramental seal has always and everywhere in the Church of Christ been most faithfully observed."[1] The sacramental seal is a divine pledge that he who is Christ's instrument in the tribunal of mercy will conceal the penitent's sins forever. "He will cast all our sins into the bottom of the sea" (*Micheas* 7, 19).

The purpose of this dissertation is to review the basic teaching concerning the sacramental seal and to examine its canonical aspects. In treating a topic of this nature, one must lean heavily on the opinions of theologians and canonists rather than on more fundamental canonical principles of interpretation. In virtue of canon 20, the common and constant teaching of the *doctores* is recognized as a supplementary norm of interpretation. There is room, however, for the application of some more basic canonical principles of interpretation, especially in regard to the penalties enacted in canon 2369.

The writer expresses his gratitude to His Excellency, the Most Reverend William A. Scully, D.D., Bishop of Albany, for the opportunity to undertake graduate studies. He is likewise grateful to the members of the Faculty and to the student priests of the School of Canon Law of The Catholic University of America for their valued association.

[1] Cf. Appendix II, p. 110.

TABLE OF CONTENTS

TABLE OF CONTENTS (Continued)

TABLE OF CONTENTS (Continued)

CHAPTER I

The Seal as Derived From Divine Law

THE DIVINE SEAL

The constant practice and thought of the Church, as well as the common teaching of theologians, shows that the sacramental seal is based on more than church law and, it must be added, on more than the natural law alone. One indication of this truth is the absolute inviolability predicated of the sacramental seal. Under certain conditions, natural and committed secrets, protected by the natural law, can be lawfully revealed even against the will of the one who entrusted the secret. But this is not true of the sacramental secret. No motive, however important, whether of a temporal or of a spiritual nature, excuses from the seal of confession; aside from the penitent himself, no authority on earth, not even the pope, has the power to dispense from its observance. This absolute inviolability indicates that sacramental secrecy has at its source more than either church law or the natural law alone.[1]

While authors agree that the seal derives from more than church law or the natural law alone, they are not unanimous in their explanation of this higher derivation. A commonly accepted explanation, however, maintains that the obligation of the seal is a natural consequence of the establishment of the sacrament of penance and is implicitly contained in the positive divine law which obliges the faithful to submit their sins to the power of the

---

[1] "Generice loquendo . . . legem sigilli esse de jure divino atque absolute inviolabilem, est tam communis et firma theologorum doctrina, ab ipsa Ecclesiae praxi et sensu roborata, ut contraria sententia hodie nec caute nec tuto sustineri queat, adeoque videatur mereri censuram propositionis *temerariae*."—Doronzo, *De Poenitentia* (4 vols., Milwaukee: Bruce, 1949-1953), II, 785.

"Obligatio servandi sigilli, etsi non semper cum ultimis suis determinationibus cognita est, tamen ita fundatur in traditione et sacramenti natura ut dici queat esse de jure divino."—Galtier, *De Paenitentia* (Editio nova, Romae: Pont. Univ. Gregoriana, 1950), p. 473.

keys. The reasoning is as follows: Christ established the sacrament of penance to be a fruitful means of salvation and sanctification; by a positive command, He directed the faithful to confess their sins. Christ's intention would be frustrated and His command would be, humanly considered, impossible of fulfillment if Christ did not also intend that the penitent's self-accusation of sins would not be turned against him in the extra-sacramental forum. Consequently, in the divine institution of the sacrament of penance as well as in the divine command to confess one's sins, there must be implied an assurance or pledge that the information revealed by the penitent in sacramental confession will not be converted to his detriment outside confession. Otherwise Christ would have established an instrument of salvation which men would have found insurmountably difficult to employ; He would have imposed an obligation and yet would have failed to provide the conditions necessary to make the fulfillment of this obligation not solely a metaphysical possibility but a possibility in view of human nature.

Since God commanded the confession of one's sins, He certainly intended the means necessary to make feasible the observance of this command. Certainly, in view of human nature, the sacramental seal is necessary for this end. Without the protection of the seal, the sacrament would lose much of its utility as an instrument of salvation. Can anyone deny that this would be alien to the intention which Christ had in establishing the sacrament of penance as an accessible and fruitful instrument of salvation? It is indeed legitimate to conclude that, even if Christ did not explicitly command confessors not to turn confessional knowledge to the extra-sacramental detriment of the penitent,[2] nevertheless, the obligation is a natural consequence of the establishment of the sacrament and is implicitly contained in Christ's command for the faithful to submit their sins to the power of the keys. "In other words, since Christ instituted the Sacrament and imposed on all the baptized the obligation of secret confession, He thereby instituted a secure means of seeking forgiveness of sin, safeguarded,

---

[2] Some theologians have maintained that the seal is based on "a *special* positive command of Christ."—Cf. Kurtscheid, *A History of the Seal of Confession* (Tr. by F. A. Marks, St. Louis: B. Herder, 1927), pp. 280-281.

that is, in the highest degree from every circumstance extrinsic to the tribunal that could possibly redound to the shame, inconvenience, or annoyance of the penitent."[3]

Many authors propose the foregoing explanation as the chief argument in demonstration of the divine source and inviolability of the seal.[4] St. Thomas (1225-1274) and others, while not accepting this as the principal explanation, none the less admitted it to be a valid, albeit secondary, proof.[5]

In summary, a necessary consequence of the establishment of

---

[3] Davis, *Moral and Pastoral Theology* (Fifth edition revised and enlarged, 4 vols., New York: Sheed and Ward, 1946), III, 317.

[4] ". . . Christus dum instituit sacramentum poenitentiae, praecepitque confessionem, simul confessariis arctissimam hanc sigilli obligationem imposuit; ut patet tum ex perpetua traditione ac sensu Ecclesiae; tum ex eo, quia alioquin praeceptum confessionis non esset accommodatum conditioni humanae, ac spirituali fidelium utilitati."—Reiffenstuel, *Theologia Moralis* (Novissime a P. Flaviano Ricci a Cimbria instaurata, 2 vols., Bassani, prostant Venetiis: Remondini, 1773), tr. 14, dist. 4, q. 3, concl. 3, n. 23.

"Lex autem sigilli sacramentalis, formaliter accepta, est *iuris positivi divini*: si enim confessarius ad sigillum servandum non adstringeretur, confessio esset impossibilis et evaderet onus prorsus intolerabile: dum ergo Dominus noster obligationem imposuit confitendi peccata quoad speciem et numerum, voluit etiam proculdubio ut a confessario peccata arctissimo sigillo tergerentur; secus dicendum esset ipsum praecepisse rem impossibilem et prorsus intolerabilem. De hac obligatione sigilli non datur in SS. Scripturis praeceptum explicitum; constat tamen ex certa constantique traditione Ecclesiae: nec desunt auctores qui tenent peculiare hoc sigilli praeceptum a Christo Domino Apostolis significatum fuisse."—Sartori in Palazzini-DeJorio, *Casus Conscientiae* (Propositi ac resoluti a pluribus theologis ac canonistis Urbis, 2 vols., Torino: Marietti, 1958), II, Casus 434, ad I, 565-566.

[5] ". . . in sacramentis ea quae exterius geruntur sunt signa rerum quae interius contingunt. Et ideo confessio qua quis sacerdoti se subiicit, signum est interioris, qua quis Deo subiicitur. Deus autem peccatum illius qui se sibi subiicit per poenitentiam, tegit. Unde et hoc oportet in sacramento poenitentiae significari. Et ideo de necessitate sacramenti est quod quis confessionem celet; et tamquam violator sacramenti peccat qui confessionem revelat. Et praeter hoc sunt aliae utilitates huius celationis: quia per hoc homines magis ad confessionem attrahuntur; et simplicius etiam peccata confitentur."—*Summa Theologica—Opera Omnia* (34 vols., Parisiis: Apud Ludovicum Vivès, 1871-1880), V, *Supplementum*, q. 11, art. 1. For an explanation of St. Thomas' principal reason, see Doronzo, *op. cit.*, II, 812-816.

the sacrament of penance and an implication in Christ's command for men to confess their sins is the divine pledge that the penitent's self-accusation will not be made to work against him extra-sacramentally. This divine pledge is, in the opinion of the writer, the seal of confession in its fulness as it derives from the divine law. It can be called the "divine seal of confession."

To outline the full scope of this divine pledge or seal, it is necessary to examine the manner in which the confessor (or others) could turn the penitent's self-accusation of sins to the disadvantage of the penitent in the extra-sacramental forum. There seem to be three general possibilities, inasmuch as the sacramental knowledge disclosed to the confessor could be perverted by him extra-sacramentally in three distinct directions or in relation to three distinct parties. These three distinct parties are: a third person (or persons); the penitent; the confessor himself. The confessor could turn the penitent's self-accusation to the penitent's detriment:

(a) by revealing it to some *third person or persons;*
(b) by speaking of it to the *penitent* outside confession;
(c) by allowing it to influence *his own* extra-sacramental actions to the disadvantage of the penitent.

Of course, by one and the same action, the confessor might possibly perpetrate not just one, but two, or even all three of these eventualities.

Christ, in establishing the sacrament of penance and in commanding the confession of sins, certainly intended that the penitent should be protected against all three categories of offenses listed above. Otherwise the sacrament would become odious to the faithful and would undoubtedly fall into widespread disuse.[6] Christ must have pledged, at least implicitly, that whatever the penitent confessed would not be turned to his disadvantage outside confession in any of the three ways mentioned. This is the seal as it

[6] ". . . memini me legisse, quod apud Abissinos, vel Aethiopes hoc sacramentum fere abiit in desuetudinem propter malitiam sacerdotum, qui sigillum religiose non observabant."—DeLugo, *De Sacramento Poenitentiae, —Disputationes Scholasticae et Morales* (Edito nova, 8 vols., Parisiis: Apud Ludovicum Vivès, 1868-1869), V, disp. 23, sect. 1, n. 4.

derives from the divine law, that is, the divine seal. It can be defined as a pledge for the penitent and a correlative obligation for the confessor and others, insuring that whatever the penitent reveals in his self-accusation of sins will not be turned against him extra-sacramentally either by revelation to a third party, by confrontation to the penitent himself, or by other displeasing use by the confessor. The divine seal, therefore, forbids:

(a) The revelation of anything disclosed to the confessor in sacramental confession, the revelation of which would be displeasing and odious to penitents. Above all else, this includes the betrayal of the sinner by revealing his identity and his sin;

(b) The confessor's speaking to the penitent outside confession about confessional matter;

(c) Any other use of confessional knowledge by the confessor if such use would be displeasing to the penitent.

POST-CODE CONTROVERSY

In the previous pages, the writer attempted to outline the extent of the obligation of the seal as it springs from the divine law. The argumentation was based on theological reasoning without any reference to the laws of the Church. It is now necessary to ascertain whether the concept of the divine seal, as explained above, can be retained in view of the Code of Canon Law.

In its chapter on the minister of the sacrament of penance, the Code includes two canons dealing with this matter, namely, canons 889 and 890. The first concerns the *proditio peccatoris,* which is understood as including the factor of revelation to a third party.[7] The second canon forbids the turning of confessional knowledge to the penitent's detriment or displeasure through uses which do not involve any revelation. Only the obligation, delineated in canon 889, of not betraying the sinner (*prodere peccatorem*) is called the seal in the Code. Consequently, the prohibition forbidding the *proditio peccatoris* is identified with the canonical use of the term "seal" and can therefore be called the "canonical seal." The prohibition of canon 890 is not called the seal in the Code

[7] Cf. *infra,* p. 15.

and, as a consequence, does not fall under the canonical seal; rather, it can be called the forbidden use of confessional knowledge.

Two questions immediately arise:

(a) Should a definition of the seal of confession as it arises from the divine law embrace not only the obligation outlined in canon 889 but also in canon 890, or should it be restricted, as the Code restricts the term, to canon 889? In short, do the obligations as stated in both of these canons convene generically, as it were, in the same divine law, or do they, as derived from the divine law, pertain to two completely distinct laws and concepts?

(b) Even if they do convene generically, should the term "seal of confession" be used in designation of this generic obligation and thereby become applicable to each specific obligation falling therein? Or should the term be reserved exclusively, as in the Code, in designation of the specific obligation set down in canon 889, some other term being adopted in signification of the more generic obligation?

Doronzo, pointing out that there are two questions involved, calls them *quaestio de ipsa re* and *quaestio de nomine.*[8]

According to their answers, post-Code authors can be classified in two groups. Some, without distinguishing the two questions, reserve the term "seal of confession" to denote the obligation enunciated in canon 889; others apply it analogously to the obligations found in canons 889 and 890. Illustrative of the first group are:

> MERKELBACH: Aliud est sigillum seu secretum servandum; aliud obligatio non utendi notitia in confessione acquisita etiam sine laesione secreti. Hoc ultimum a quibusdam parum accurate vocatur sigillum accidentale; imo multi de utroque simul tractant promiscue et sine distinctione. Oportet tamen ea distinguere: sigillum nempe valde strictius obligat quam alterum:[9]
>
> KURTSCHEID: The two offences, the violation of the sacramental Seal and the abuse of sacramental knowledge, differ widely from each other, and in the same manner as we have treated them separately in our treatise, so also has the new Code clearly distinguished between both.

[8] De Paenitentia, II, 832-836.

[9] *Summa Theologiae Moralis* (Editio octava aucta et emendata, 3 vols., Montreal: Desclee de Brouwer, 1949), III, n. 621, p. 582, nota 1.

> Some authors have not adverted to this and defined the Seal of Confession in a manner which excluded every use of the knowledge obtained in confession "cum gravamine poenitentis." Even since the publication of the new Code this difference has not been noted by all canonists.[10]

> REGATILLO: Codex clare distinguit inter sigillum (c. 889, 2.369), et usum notitiae ex confessione habitae.[11]

As these texts show, the principal argument of those who consider it incorrect to apply the term "seal of confession" to the forbidden use of confessional knowledge rests on the fact that the Code, treating the revelation of confession and the forbidden use of confessional knowledge in separate canons, applies the term only to the former and not to the latter.

A second class of authors indeed distinguishes between the revelation of confession and the forbidden use of confessional knowledge. But the distinction is one made within the seal itself and not a distinction between the seal and a second, independent law or concept. According to this second opinion, the law of the seal embraces not only the obligation outlined in canon 889 but also the obligation spelled out in canon 890. Consequently, these authors maintain that the term "seal of confession" can, in accordance with the traditional usage, be predicated analogously, but none the less properly, of both obligations. These authors allow a twofold acceptance of the term, giving it two proper definitions, one broad, the other strict, but both proper. In its broad acceptance, the term can be predicated of the obligations stated in both canon 889 and canon 890. Both analogously fall within the seal. But inasmuch as the Code uses the term only with reference to the foremost of the two obligations, namely, that which is outlined in canon 889, the term in its strict acceptance can be reserved exclusively for the contents of canon 889. Illustrative of this opinion are the following:

> Conte a CORONATA: Aliqui moderniores, ad clariorem intelligentiam quaestionum circa hanc materiam agitatarum, distinguunt duplicem acceptionem vocis sigilli

---

[10] *A History of the Seal of Confession*, pp. 309-310.

[11] *Ius Sacramentarium* (Editio secunda, Santander: Sal Terrae, 1949), n. 547, p. 318.

sacramentalis, scilicet *sigillum sensu stricto* et *sigillum sensu lato* acceptum. *Sigillum sensu stricto* est strictissima obligatio servandi secretum et abstinendi ab omni usu extrasacramentali, invito poenitente, circa omnia quae idem poenitens in ordine ad sacramentalem absolutionem obtinendam dixit, quorum manifestatio vel usus poenitentem proderet, aut saltem suspicionem audientibus vel videntibus ingereret.—*Sigillum vero sensu lato* acceptum est strictissima obligatio abstinendi ab usu notitiae habitae ex confessione sacramentali, cuius manifestatio vergeret in odium Sacramenti aut in gravamen poenitentis, etiam pro casu quo nullum revelationis periculum adsit.

Huiusmodi distinctio sigilli retineri potest, quia apta videtur ad melius explicandos varios casus occurrentes et deinde etiam quia in Codice fundamentum habet (Cfr. cc. 889 et 890).[12]

It is interesting to note Conte a Coronata's claim that the Code furnishes foundation for distinguishing two significations of the seal—strict and broad. It was on this same basis that the prior opinion reserved the term exclusively for canon 889.

DAVIS: The seal may and should also be understood in a wider sense, namely, inasmuch as it is forbidden in the canons for a confessor not only to reveal confessional matter but to use his knowledge of it outside the Sacrament, against the will of the penitent, so as to render the Sacrament of confession in any way burdensome or odious. Consequently, every use of confessional knowledge that is irksome to a penitent, even if there is no danger of revealing anything, is contrary to the obligation of the seal in the wider sense of the term.[13]

DORONZO: Cum enim sigillum importet conceptum analogicum, non alia assignari potest definitio quam ea quae convenit talibus conceptibus, qua nampe exprimatur conceptus unus, sed unitate quadam confusionis et proportionis . . . genericus conceptus sigilli dividitur in duos determinatos conceptus seu modos se habendi ad celationem confessionis, i.e., non proditionem peccatoris, cui ratio celationis perfecte et simpliciter convenit, tamquam principali analogato, et non usum scientiae sacra-

---

[12] *Institutiones Iuris Canonici* (5 vols., Vol. I-IV editio quarta aucta et emendata; Vol. V, ed. 3; Taurini: Marietti, 1950-1955), IV, n. 2129, pp. 619-620, et nota 2.

[13] *Moral and Pastoral Theology,* III, 316.

> mentalis cum gravamine peccatoris, cui ratio celationis convenit tantummodo imperfecte et secundum quid tamquam secundario analogato.[14]

Doronzo devotes several pages to an exposition of the reasons for his opinion.[15] It will be profitable to present a brief summary of these reasons. Doronzo, as mentioned before, maintains that two questions are at issue in this controversy—*quaestio de nomine et quaestio de ipsa re*. The first of these, the question of terminology, must be settled primarily on an examination of the usage. In the writings of theologians, the term "sacramental seal" in its proper signification was constantly applied to the prohibition forbidding the use of confessional knowledge against the penitent. The mediaeval dispute concerning the lawfulness of using such knowledge *cum gravamine poenitentis* centered on the question of whether or not such use would or would not constitute a violation of the seal in its proper sense. After the dispute was resolved, theologians treated this prohibited use of confessional knowledge under the rubric of the *sigillum* and generally classified its use as an indirect violation of the seal in its proper sense. Doronzo cites modern theologians who have continued to call the unlawful use of sacramental knowledge a violation of the seal. And even from the ranks of those modern authors who reserve the term "seal" exclusively for the obligation of non-revelation, there are found those who, in their treatment of the prohibited use of confessional knowledge, are unable to depart completely from the traditional manner of considering and arranging this matter. Cappello, for example, asserts that the proper meaning of the seal and the only meaning accepted by him is the seal in its strict sense, that is, as applicable to canon 889 exclusively. In spite of this assertion, however, he treats the obligation of canon 890 as well as that of canon 889 in his chapter *"De Sigillo Sacramentali."* In that same chapter he considers the violation of canon 890 under the article *"De violatione sigilli."*[16]

---

[14] *De Poenitentia*, II, 835-836.

[15] Cf. *op. cit.*, II, 831-836.

[16] Cf. Doronzo, *op. cit.*, II, 833-834. Cf. also Cappello, *Tractatus Canonico-Moralis de Sacramentis* (Vols. I, II, V, 6. ed.; III, IV, 3. ed., Taurini: Marietti, 1949-1953), II, n. 583, p. 602, and n. 614, p. 630.

According to Doronzo, the Code, by using the term "seal" in canon 889 and not in canon 890, determines the canonical sense of that term. But it does not rule out the accepted and traditional usage of theologians whereby, in theology, unlawful use of confessional knowledge has been called a violation of the seal in its proper sense. The Code does not intend to determine the theological sense and usage of words. The reason why the Code seems to reserve the term for canon 889 is that this canon enunciates the principal object of the seal. In addition, this reservation of the term helps to prevent confusion in interpreting the canons. Finally, Doronzo maintains that a second acceptation of the term is not foreign to the mind of the Code:

> Ceterum in Codice sermo de usu scientiae (can. 890) submittitur immediate sermoni de proditioni peccatoris (can. 889) velut quaedam continuatio ejusdem legis secreti sacramentalis; praeterea, in can. 1757, § 3, n. 2, Codex videtur pro objecto sigilli habere "ea omnia quae ipsis [sacerdotibus] ex confessione sacramentali innotuerunt" (ut suadent verba immediate sequentia "Etsi vinculo sigilli soluti sint"), jamvero non omnia quae acquiruntur scientia sacramentali sunt objectum sigilli stricte dicti, sed quaedam constituunt objectum merae scientiae sacramentalis; praeterea, in Indice Codicis usus scientiae sacramentalis (can. 890) refertur una cum ipsa proditione peccatoris (can. 889) sub eadem communi voce "sigilli sacramentalis." Quae omnia ostendunt alteram acceptionem vocis sigilli non esse alienam a mente Codicis.[17]

Doronzo turns from the *quaestio de nomine* to the *quaestio de ipsa re*. Even if the term "seal" would be determined in future documents of the Church as applicable solely to the principal object of the sacramental secret, namely, the *non-proditio peccatoris*, there would still remain the primary question, *quaestio de ipsa re*. Do the obligations set forth in canons 889 and 890 pertain to the same law and concept, so that they might properly be signified by means of the same term, whatever that might be? Doronzo contends that the non-revelation or concealment of the sinner and

[17] *Op. cit.*, II, 834.

the non-use of sacramental knowledge *cum gravamine poenitentis* are reducible to the same concept, although analogously, and pertain substantially to the same law:

> Id autem ostenditur *primo,* ex consideratione indolis duarum illarum obligationum; utraque enim refertur ad peccatorum confessionem et importat quandam illius obsignationem, cautelam et protectionem ab indebita aliorum usurpatione, quamvis diverso modo, quia per celationem peccata obsignantur et proteguntur ab indebita cognitione, per prohibitionem vero usus scientiae sacramentalis proteguntur ab indebita actione fundata in ipsa licita cognitione. *Secundo,* id ostenditur ex consideratione fundamenti ex quo illae obligationes oriuntur; utraque enim fundatur in ipsa indole hujus sacramenti, seu oritur ex triplici necessitate se conformandi tum significationi sacramentali, tum indoli ministri, tum fini sacramenti. *Tertio,* id ostenditur ex modo quo lex secreti sacramentalis pedetemptim per saecula evoluta est in doctrina theologorum et propositione auctoritatis ecclesiasticae; manifeste enim apparet eandem legem sigilli ex strictiori conceptu celationis peccatoris sese extendisse ad prohibitionem gravosi usus scientiae sacramentalis, tamquam in homogeneum et connaturale suum complementum.[18]

OPINION OF THE WRITER

Quaestio de ipsa re: In the opinion of the writer, not only the obligation expressed in canon 889 but also that of canon 890 is prohibited by the seal as it derives from the divine law. Both obligations fall under the divine seal. The primary argument urging this opinion is that the theological reasoning previously outlined to show how the obligation of the seal springs from the divine law, reasoning generally accepted by theologians either as their principal explanation or at least a valid secondary one, applies without contortions not only to the obligation enunciated in canon 889 but also to that outlined in canon 890.

Secondly, throughout those centuries when the extent of the obligation of the seal was being probed by theologians, they con-

[18] *Op. cit.,* II, 835.

stantly considered the question of the forbidden use of confessional knowledge as a question proper to the seal. In the common opinion of pre-Code theologians, the obligation of the seal extended beyond that which today is set down in canon 889. They taught, for example, that the *seal* forbids the confessor to speak to the penitent of sins confessed, except in subsequent confessions or with the penitent's permission. But, as will be seen in a later chapter, this illicit action on the part of the confessor would not violate the law enacted in canon 889.[19] Just this one example illustrates that the traditional pre-Code view of theologians considered the extent of the seal as encompassing more than the *non-proditio peccatoris* mentioned in canon 889.[20]

Does the Code prove that the traditional pre-Code view was incorrect? The writer believes such an assertion would be reading more into the Code than it is certain the legislator intended. Is it not conceivable that the legislator had no intention of correcting the theological notion of the seal, but merely wished to make clear that part of the divine seal which, being the principal obligation, but not necessarily the exclusive obligation of the divine seal, the Church wished to specify as the seal in canonical usage and to fortify with canonical sanctions? If that had been the intention of the legislator, could he not have written in exactly the same manner as he has written in the Code? Could he not have intended to determine the strict, canonical use of the term without also intending to correct the commonly accepted pre-Code view of theologians concerning the seal? To say that he intended more is, in the writer's opinion, without foundation. As Doronzo points

---

[19] Cf. *infra*, p. 77.

[20] Long before the Code, an author saw the need of distinguishing the seal in the strict sense from the seal in the broad sense. It was in the second category that he placed the confessor's obligation not to speak extra-sacramentally to the penitent of sins confessed: "Aliquibus tamen placuit opinio Hurtad . . . ubi tenet dictam locutionem [cum poenitente] non esse contra sigillum stricte sumptum, quia non est apertio secreti stricte sumpti . . . esse tamen contra sigillum late sumptum . . ."—Diana, *Resolutiones Morales* (Coordinati per V. P. Martinum de Alcolea, editio novissima, 10 vols., Venetiis: Ex typographia Balleoniana, 1728), I, tr. 8, "De Sigillo Confessionis," resol. 58.

out, even the composer of the Code's Index must have failed to detect any further intention in the mind of the legislator.[21]

The two reasons just stated seem sufficient to the writer to support the view that the obligation not only as stated in canon 889 but also as outlined in canon 890 falls under the sacramental seal as it derives from divine law.

Quaestio de nomine: Authors seem justified in calling the obligation enunciated in canon 889 the *"sigillum stricte dictum"* and the one outlined in canon 890 the *"sigillum late dictum."* Such a distinction, on the one hand, honors the fact that the Code uses the term "seal" only in reference to canon 889 and, on the other hand, retains the general pre-Code usage which predicated the term of both obligations. One author objects to using the term "seal" in reference to canon 890 on the grounds that its violation would thereby be subject to the penalties of canon 2369. In his words, "this conclusion will not be accepted even by those who give a wide definition of the seal."[22] This argument does not seem to rule out the use of the terms, "seal in its strict sense" and "seal in its broad sense," inasmuch as canon 19 demands that terms which are used in both a strict and a broad sense must be accepted in their narrower meaning whenever penalties are under consideration.

For several reasons, however, the writer prefers to use the term "canonical seal" in place of the phrase "seal in its strict sense," and to employ the expression "forbidden use of confessional knowledge" rather than the phrase "seal in its broad sense." First, at least the "canonical seal" is a more compact and manageable expression than the "seal in its strict sense." Secondly, the "canonical seal" by the words themselves indicates the seal as it is defined in the *Code of Canon Law.* Thirdly, "forbidden use

---

[21] ". . . in Indice Codicis usus scientiae sacramentalis (can. 890) refertur una cum ipsa proditione peccatoris (can. 889) sub eadem communi voce 'sigilli sacramentalis.' "—*op. cit.,* II, 834. ". . . the alphabetical index . . . was compiled by an expert canonist, Father Ojetti, S.J., of the Gregorian University"—Bouscaren-Ellis, *Canon Law* (Second revised edition, Milwaukee: Bruce, 1955), p. 6.

[22] McCarthy, *Problems in Theology,* Vol. I, *The Sacraments* (Westminster, Md.: Newman Press, 1956), p. 252.

of confessional knowledge" is a phrase formulated from the actual terminology of canon 890. Finally, the terms when thus chosen designate more sharply which of the two canons is under consideration and clarify the treatment of the penalties enacted in canon 2369. As already mentioned, the writer believes that the obligations enunciated in both canon 889 and canon 890 pertain to the same fundamental obligation as derived from the divine law, that is, to the divine seal.

CHAPTER II

The Seal as Defined in Canon 889

Canon 889, § 1, explains the canonical use of the term "seal of confession" or "sacramental seal." It is the seal as defined in this canon that the writer has in mind when he speaks of the "canonical seal." It is thereby readily distinguished from the broader notion of the "divine seal."[1] The use of the term "canonical seal" must not be interpreted as an implication that the contents of canon 889 are based only on church law and not on divine law. Rather, it means to specify that part of the divine law of the seal which the church has expressly called the seal in its legal sense and has fortified with penal sanctions.

PRODITIO PECCATORIS

Canon 889 defines the seal as an obligation prohibiting the *proditio peccatoris* ("*Caveat ne prodat peccatorem*"). To understand the notion of the canonical seal, it is necessary and sufficient to examine the phrase *proditio peccatoris* in its legal meaning. The wording of canon 889, § 1, is derived from the decree *Omnis utriusque sexus* of the IV General Council of the Lateran (1215). This derivation is plainly evident from a juxtaposing of the two texts:

> CANON 889, § 1: Sacramentale sigillum inviolabile est; quare *caveat diligenter confessarius ne verbo aut signo*

[1] Cf. *supra*, pp. 1-5. P. Rota (+ 1879) indicated a somewhat similar distinction when he wrote: "Juxta hunc sensum, qui *secundum ius divinum* appellatur, ad distinctionem prioris, qui secundum *ius ecclesiasticum nuncupatur,* communiter Theologi definiunt violationem sigilli."— *Enchiridion Confessarii et Judicis Ecclesiastici* (Augustae Taurinorum: Petrus Marietti, 1884), pars. 1, sect. 1, cap. 5, n. 49. Ballerini (1805-1881) employed the same distinction when he wrote: ". . . alius secundum ius ecclesiasticum, alius secundum ius divinum de sigillo judicat . . ." Ballerini's annotations as found in Gury, *Compendium Theologiae Moralis* (Editio decima, Antonii Ballerini adnotationibus locupletatum, 2 vols., Romae: Ex typographia S. C. de Propaganda Fide, 1887-1889), II, n. 666, nota (a).

> *aut alio quovis modo et quavis de causa prodat aliquatenus peccatorem.*
>
> "OMNIS UTRIUSQUE SEXUS": *Caveat autem omnino, ne verbo, vel signo, vel alio quovis modo prodat aliquatenus peccatorem;* sed si prudentiori consilio indiguerit, illud absque ulla expressione personae caute requirat: quoniam qui peccatum in poenitentiali judicio sibi detectum praesumpserit revelare, non solum a sacerdotali officio deponendum decernimus, verum etiam ad agendam perpetuam poenitentiam in arctum monasterium detrudendam.[2]

If the reader hunts through the footnotes in the Code to canon 889, § 1, he will not find any reference to the above-quoted decree of the Lateran Council. However, the text from the Lateran Council passed into the *Compilatio Quarta* of the *Quinque Compilationes Antiquae* and from there into the *Gregorian Decretals.*[3] In the footnote to canon 889, § 1, the Decretal citation is found. Consequently, the decree of the IV General Council of the Lateran is among the *fontes* of canon 889, not directly, but via the Decretals.

Canon 889, § 1, as well as *Omnis utriusque sexus* of the Lateran Council, speaks of the *proditio peccatoris. Caveat ne prodat peccatorem* is found in both texts. While canon 889 does not define the expression, the Lateran decree does determine the legal meaning of the phrase. It explains the *proditio peccatoris* as the revelation of a sin known from confession ("qui peccatum in poenitentiali judicio sibi detectum praesumpserit revelare"). One element, therefore, found in the notion of *proditio peccatoris* is the revelation of a sin known from confession. Is this the sole requisite for a betrayal of the sinner, a *proditio peccatoris?* A further examination of the Lateran decree forces the conclusion that a mere revelation of the sin without the identification of the sinner does not constitute a *proditio peccatoris.* This conclusion is justified by the

---

[2] Cap. 21—Mansi, *Sacrorum Conciliorum Nova et Amplissima Collectio* (53 vols., Parisiis, 1901-1927), XXII, 1007-1010.

[3] C. 12, X, *de poenitentiis et remissionibus,* V, 38. "This ordinance of the Fourth Lateran Council passed into the compilation known as *'Compilatio Quarta.'* . . . From this compilation Raymond of Peñaforte took the canon into the Decretals."—Kurtscheid, *A History of the Seal of Confession,* pp. 117-118.

provision made in that same text for the confessor to seek "more prudent advice" concerning a confession if this is deemed necessary by him. He is free to do so provided the identity of the penitent is not disclosed (*sed si prudentiori consilio indiguerit, illud absque ulla expressione personae caute requirat*). It is legitimate to conclude, therefore, that the *proditio peccatoris* consists of the revelation in a conjunctive manner of both the sin confessed and the sinner who confessed it.

> Peccata ipsa sine expressione personae non cadunt sub sigillum confessionis; nam sigillum confessionis est juris divini, ita, ut nemo praeter poenitentem in illo dispensare possit, ut docent communiter TT et canonistae; atqui circa revelationem peccati dispensat concilium generale, *c. cit.* et statuit, licere sacerdoti consilii causa revelare alteri peccatum, quod in confessione audiit; igitur dicto *cap.* solum prohibetur revelatio peccati in confessione auditi per ordinem, et relationem ad confitentem, quando scilicet ita revelatur peccatum, ut exinde etiam is, qui peccavit, noscatur; talis autem non est, cum e.g. aliquis dicit: *tale, vel tale peccatum mortale audivi in confessione.*[4]

This notion of *proditio peccatoris* can be corroborated and clarified by way of a brief look at texts from several authors, especially those texts which deal with the pre-Code penalty established for confessors who betrayed the sinner by revealing him and his sin. The *proditio peccatoris* by the confessor constituted a delict in pre-Code legislation, as is evident from the penalty specified in the Lateran decree. It remains a delict in the law of the Code, the penalty being established in canon 2369. While the penalty was changed in the Code, the nature of the delict, the notion of *proditio peccatoris,* was not altered. The offense remains the same; only the sanction differs. Consequently, an examination of the conditions postulated for the incurring of the penalty under the old law will serve to confirm the notion of *proditio peccatoris* derived from *Omnis utriusque sexus* of the IV General Council

[4] Schmalzgrueber, *Jus Ecclesiasticum Universum in Quinque Libros Decretalium Gregorii IX* (5 vols. in 12, Romae: Ex typographia Rev. Cam. Apostolicae, 1843-1845), Lib. V, tit. 38, n. 74.

of the Lateran. "Although other penalties have been substituted for the older ones, nevertheless the presuppositions for these penalties are stated in the same words in which the Fourth Lateran Council couched them. Therefore a close examination of the older penal paragraphs will contribute not a little towards understanding the discipline now in vogue."[5]

According to De Lugo (1583-1660), the penalty enacted in the IV General Council of the Lateran was to be inflicted on a priest who revealed a sin known from confession.[6] De Lugo, however, had previously affirmed that it was not a violation of the seal to reveal a sin if the sinner was in no way identified.[7] To incur the penalty, that is, to be guilty of a *proditio peccatoris,* therefore, it was necessary to reveal both the sin and the sinner. But if a confessor were to disclose that, in some small locality, crimes such as sodomy or usury were perpetrated, would this be considered a *proditio peccatoris?* De Lugo pointed out that in such a case, when there was a question of a small locality and of sins which were not publicly known, such action would indeed be detrimental to each individual in that tiny community. But he went on to add that, in the opinion of many authors, such a disclosure on the part of the confessor would not render him liable to the penalties established for those who reveal a confession. Their argument was that the confessor would not be guilty of revealing the sin in relation to the sinner, but rather in relation to the community.[8] In the minds of these authors, therefore, to verify the notion of *prodere peccatorem* it was necessary to reveal conjointly both the sin and the sinner.

---

[5] Kurtscheid, *op. cit.,* p. 303.

[6] "Hanc poenam incurrit . . . sacerdos, qui ex confessione audita, revelat peccatum poenitentis formaliter, vel aequivalenter: ut, si dicat: Non potui illum absolvere, etc."—*Disputationes Scholasticae et Morales,* V, *De Sacramento Poenitentiae,* disp. 23, sect. 5, n. 147.

[7] "Octavo dubitatur, an liceat referre peccatum, non nominando personam poenitentis. Patentur omnes, id licere, dummodo non sit periculum ut in poenitentis suspicionem veniri possit."—*Ibid.,* sect. 3, n. 63.

[8] "Advertunt tamen, multi, non incurri hac de causa poenas revelantis confessionem: quia non manifestantur peccata poenitentis, sed civitatis, de quo videri possunt plures, quos affert Diana I, tom. tr. I. miscell. resol. 13."—*Ibid.,* sect. 3, n. 64.

Further precision concerning the notion of *proditio peccatoris* was afforded by Reiffenstuel (1642-1703), Schmalzgrueber (1663-1735) and Wernz (1842-1914) in their expositions of the conditions which were required in pre-Code legislation before penalties for violations of the seal were to be inflicted, that is, before one was to be considered guilty of a *proditio peccatoris.*

Reiffenstuel listed several conditions which had to be fulfilled before the penalty was to be inflicted. Among the conditions were the following:

> Requiritur, ut sacerdos revelet verum aliquod mortale vel veniale peccatum in specie v.g. homicidii, jactantiae, vel in genere dicat, talem confessum fuisse peccatum mortale; . . . c. *Omnis,* etc. ubi de solis peccatis fit mentio, consequenter de solis illis intelligenda venit iuris dispositio; hinc licet illi, qui alia etsi alias sub sigillum cadentia, veluti defectus natalium, vel aliud quidpiam probrosum, aut praejudiciosum poenitenti revelant, gravissime peccent, gravique arbitraria iudicis et quidem graviori poena plectendi sint, quam violantes sacretum naturale, ordinariae tamen poenae violantis sigillum non subiacent. . . . Requiritur, ut quis peccatum non ipsi poenitenti peracta confessione, extra illam sine ipsius licentia objiciat, sed alicui alteri revelet; quia revelare proprie non dicitur nisi is qui secretum sibi commissum alteri prodit; quare extra confessionem objiciens peccatum ipsi poenitenti, ordinariae poenae non subiacet, sed extraordinariae duntaxat.[9]

In similar fashion, Schmalzgrueber enumerated the prerequisites for incurring the pre-Code penalties established for any confessor who presumed to betray the penitent. These prerequisites included the following:

> Ut vero poenis praedictis locus sit, DD. exigunt . . . ut revelet peccatum; nam si aliud quidpiam, quod sub sigillum cadit, in confessione delectum revelet, e.g. defectum natalium, vel aliud quidpiam poenitenti ignominiosum,

[9] Reiffenstuel, *Jus Canonicum Universum* (Juxta novissimam Romanam Editionem R. D. Victoris Pelletier, 7 vols., Parisiis: Apud Ludovicum Vivès, 1864-1870), Lib. 5, tit. 38, nn. 6-8.

arbitraria solum, multo tamen graviori poena, quam violans secretum naturale, puniri debet . . . [et] ut peccatum revelet alteri; nam si ipsi poenitenti obiiciantur; cum haec obiectio proprie revelatio non sit, iterum extraordinariae duntaxat poenae [puniri debet].[10]

On this same subject, Wernz can be profitably quoted, as follows:

Sacerdos, qui *peccatum* ex sola *confessione* sacramentali cognitum *tertiae* personae a poenitente distinctae *praesumptuose* revelat, *per sententiam ferendam* affligendus est poenae depositionis a sacerdotali officio. . . . Quodsi . . . non peccatum, sed alius defectus in confessione detectus in gravamen poenitentis publicetur, aut peccatum quidem manifestetur, at ipsi poenitenti, non tertiae personae . . . *ordinariae* poenae violationis sigilli sacramentalis in iure statutae non sunt applicandae.[11]

From these texts of Reiffenstuel, Schmalzgrueber, and Wernz, the following conclusions can be drawn:

(a) The pre-Code penalties for the confessor who violated the sacramental seal were not applicable unless, among other things, he revealed a sin (as distinguished from something else of an odious nature known from confession) to a third party (as distinguished from speaking of the sin to the penitent outside of confession).

(b) Since the pre-Code delict to which these penalties were attached consisted in the *proditio peccatoris,* these conditions, that is, revelation of a sin to a third party, are essential to the notion of *proditio peccatoris.*

(c) Consequently, these same elements are required for a violation of the seal as it is defined in canon 889, § 1, that is, for a violation of the canonical seal.

Other pre-Code authors wrote in a similar vein:

Duplici modo, prout in antecessum decuimus (§ 50), sumitur violatio sigilli. Prior, qui nuncupatur juxta jus ecclesiasticum, quippe qui ad poenas ordinarias in jure

[10] *Op. cit.,* Lib. V, tit. 38, n. 80.

[11] *Ius Decretalium* (6 vols., Prati: Ex officina libraria Giachetti, 1898-1914), VI, n. 466.

ecclesiastico statutas requiritur, strictior est, et violationem sigilli in hoc consistere definit, ut si *revelatio, tum peccati, tum peccatoris temerario a Sacerdote, qui confessionem sacramentalem excepit, alicui extra poenitentem facta.* Dixi 1° *revelatio tum peccati, tum peccatoris.* Nam praecipua materia et objectum sigilli est peccatum. . . . Nec sufficit quod reveletur peccatum, sed opus est, ut seu directe, seu indirecte peccator ipse prodatur, quia licitum est, seclusa quavis revelatione poenitentis, loqui de eius peccatis in confessione manifestatis. . . . Ratio omnium horum est, quia in toties cit. Cap. *Omnis utriusque de Poenit. et Remiss.* cavetur dumtaxat, ne aliquatenus prodatur peccator peccatum eius revelando.[12]

. . . alii dicant fractionem sigilli adesse solum in revelatione peccati et personae, quando et poenae latae in revelantes confessionem incurruntur; alii vero etiam quando non incurruntur quidem hae poenae, sed nihilominus per revelationem quampiam aliquid sequitur in iniuriam sacramenti et in gravamen poenitentis.[13]

From these two passages, the conclusion is again reached that the pre-Code penalties for violators of the seal were not to be inflicted, and, consequently, the notion of *proditio peccatoris* was not fully verified, unless there was disclosure to a third person of both the identity of the sinner and the sin which he confessed.

Post-Code authors can also be cited who understand the betrayal of the sinner, the *proditio peccatoris* of canon 889, § 1, as embodying the same elements. It will suffice to quote three such authors:

CHRETIEN: Obligatio non prodendi poenitentem est sigillum sacramentale proprie dictum. . . . Obligatio sigilli sacramentalis adest tantum, quando revelatio eorum quae per confessionem cognita sunt poenitentem sit *proditura*: i.e. hac revelatione 1. persona poenitentis sufficenter apud alios *designatur,* et quidem 2. tamquam *peccator,* ita ut ab aliis saltem supponi possit tanquam is qui opus malum, determinatum vel non, patravit.[14]

---

[12] P. Rota, *Enchiridion Confessarii et Iudicis Ecclesiastici,* pars. 1, sect. 1, cap. 6, n. 65.

[13] Ballerini-Palmieri, *Opus Theologicum Morale* (7 vols., Prati: Giachetti, 1889-1893), V, tr. 10 sect. 5, cap. 3, n. 996.

[14] *De Sigillo Sacramentali—De Poenitentia* (Metis: Ex typis Imprimerie Lorraine, 1929), pp. 95-97.

REGATILLO: Proprie [sigillum sacramentale] est obligatio secreto servandi omnia per confessionem sacramentalem cognita, quorum revelatio peccatum simul et poenitentem prodere possint.[15]

MERKELBACH: Iamvero, teste can. 889: "sacramentale sigillum inviolabile est; quare caveat diligenter confessarius ne verbo aut signo aut alio quovis modo et quavis de causa prodat aliquatenus peccatorem" i.e. personam et peccatum.[16]

At this point it may be helpful to summarize what has been written thus far concerning the canonical seal:

(a) With the expression "canonical seal," the writer intends the sacramental seal as it is defined in the Code, namely, in canon 889, § 1.

(b) Canon 889, § 1, defines the seal in terms of an inviolable obligation prohibiting the betrayal of the sinner (*proditio peccatoris*).

(c) To understand the notion of the canonical seal, therefore, it is necessary and sufficient to examine the meaning of *proditio peccatoris.*

(d) In pre-Code law, *proditio peccatoris* meant the disclosure to a third party of both the sinner and his sin. That these elements were essential to the notion of *proditio peccatoris* is demonstrable from an examination of the canon *Omnis utriusque sexus* of the IV General Council of the Lateran together with the interpretation given by pre-Code authors. This legislation of the Lateran Council, as incorporated into the *Decretals,* remained in force until the time of the Code.[17]

(e) The *proditio peccatoris* of canon 889 must be understood in the same sense as it was understood in pre-Code legislation. Not only does the Code give no indication that the meaning has been

---

[15] *Ius Sacramentarium,* n. 547, p. 318.

[16] *Summa Theologiae Moralis,* III, n. 621, p. 582.

[17] "Hoc ius [i.e., Concilii Lateranensis] hucusque . . . viguit."—Chelodi, *Jus Canonicum de Delictis et Poenis* (Editio V, recognita et aucta a Pio Ciprotti, Vicenza: Società Anonima Tipografica fra Cattolici Vincentini, 1943), n. 92, p. 138. "Hoc ius . . . usque ad Codicem viguit."—Cappello, *Tractatus Canonico-Moralis de Censuris* (Editio quarta emendata et aucta, Taurini: Marietti, 1950), n. 196, p. 182.

altered, but rather it uses in canon 889, § 1, an almost identical wording with that found in the *Omnis utriusque sexus* of the Lateran Council. Furthermore, whenever the law of the Code certainly or even doubtfully reiterates or agrees with the pre-Code law, canon 6 demands that it be interpreted in the light of the old law. Finally, to enlarge the meaning of *proditio peccatoris* would be to extend the penalty of canon 2369. There seems to be no justification for doing so.

(f) Consequently, the *proditio peccatoris,* or, in other words, the seal as defined in canon 889, § 1, the canonical seal, can be defined as the obligation not to betray the sinner, that is, not to reveal to a third party in a conjunctive way both the identity of the sinner and the sin he confessed.

SEAL PRESUPPOSES SACRAMENTAL CONFESSION

The IV General Council of the Lateran in its classical text on the seal of confession indicated that the confessor must observe secrecy concerning sins manifested to him *in poenitentiali judicio.* The seal, as it derives from the divine law as well as from canon law, presupposes sacramental confession. The obligation to observe the seal arises from every sacramental confession and only from sacramental confession.[18]

Sacramental confession is defined as the self-accusation of one's sins to a competent priest for the sake of absolution.[19] Confession can be sacramental and thereby give rise to the obligation of the seal even though contrition, absolution, and/or satisfaction are lacking. Consequently:

(a) It is impossible to bind the priest under the seal of con-

[18] "Regula certa et communis est, oriri [sigillum] ex omni et sola confessione sacramentali."—Suarez, *De Poenitentia—Opera Omnia* (Editio nova, 28 vols. in 30, Parisiis: Apud Ludovicum Vivès, 1856-1878), XXII, disp. 33, sect. 2, n. 1.

[19] "Confessio sacramentalis est accusatio propriorum peccatorum a poenitente facta sacerdoti competenti, ad eorum absolutionem obtinendam."—Regatillo-Zalba, *Theologiae Moralis Summa* (3 vols., Matriti: Biblioteca de Autores Cristianos, 1952-1954), III, n. 532, p. 397. The question whether the "competent priest" includes a priest without the necessary jurisdiction or a layman posing as a priest will be discussed in a later chapter. Cf. *infra,* p. 50.

fession if there is no sacramental confession. "To bind a priest under the seal of confession without actual confession and with no intention of asking for absolution is a mode of speech only, for confessional secrecy does not then arise."[20] Thus, if a person manifests his conscience to a priest, who is his confessor, not however to obtain absolution but solely for some other motive, such as obtaining advice, consolation or encouragement, the priest is not bound by the seal. On the other hand, advice sought during confession can fall under the seal.

(b) If it is certain that someone, without the intention of receiving the sacrament, makes a simulated confession, solely, for example, to deceive, ridicule or seduce the confessor, the latter is not bound by the seal.[21]

(c) Should the confession be interrupted before absolution is conferred, or should absolution be denied or postponed, the confessor would still contract the obligation of the seal.

(d) The obligation of the seal arises in a sacramental confession even though the penitent were to realize his lack of proper dispositions or were intentionally to conceal a serious sin. Sacrilegious confessions, no less than fruitful confessions, give rise to the seal.

---

[20] Davis, *Moral and Pastoral Theology,* III, 318.

[21] "Hinc infertur, quando poenitens confitetur sine ulla intentione absolutionis obtinendae, non oriri sigilli obligationem. . . . Unde, licet ipse poenitens protestetur, se loqui sub sigillo, nihil refert, si vere constat non accedere ad finem obtinendi absolutionem; quod, vel ex ipsius dictis constare potest, vel ex factis, si appareat, accessisse solum animo inducendi confessarium ad aliquod peccatum."—De Lugo, *De Sacramento Poenitentiae,* disp. 23, sect. 2, n. 43.

CHAPTER III

Matter Guarded by the Seal Against Revelation

What facts or information is the confessor or others who are bound by the divine law of the seal obliged not to reveal under any circumstances without the penitent's permission? Authors have followed a fairly uniform pattern in answering this question. A few items are disputed by the authors, but most are generally accepted. This chapter will present a résumé of both the certain and the disputed matter or objects of the divine seal.

Two warnings must be given before any discussion about the matter or objects included under the seal. First, the reader must keep in mind that some facts or information, while not protected by the seal, might very well be the matter of natural and/or committed secrets. Inasmuch as the seal does not forbid the revelation of some particular items of knowledge, it is not legitimate to conclude that the confessor is free to disclose it. It is often possible that the information is protected by natural or committed secrecy.[1]

Secondly, in certain cases authors dispute whether this or that particular item falls under the seal. Although points are disputed, authors are unanimous in teaching that probabilism cannot be employed in resolving questions concerning the sacramental seal.[2]

---

[1] "Omnia quae in confessione dicuntur, quamvis fortasse non cadunt sub lege sigilli, semper tamquam *secreta saltem commissa* consideranda sunt; quae si ullo modo revelantur (etiamsi sint tantum bona desideria, charismata et virtutes) *graviter* laeditur ius poenitentis nisi *expresse* constet de eius contraria intentione."—Genicot-Salsmans, *Institutiones Theologiae Moralis* (Editio decimaseptima quam paravit A. Gortebecke, 2 vols., Bruxellis: L'Édition Universelle S.A., 1951), II, n. 365, pp. 256-257.

[2] According to probabilism one is allowed to follow an opinion favoring liberty as long as it is well-founded and then even though the opinion favoring the law be more probable. Probabiliorism demands that the law be observed unless the opinion favoring liberty be more probable than that which favors the law. These moral systems cannot be applied in matters of the seal. As long as the opinion favoring the law of the seal is well-founded and solidly probable, it must be followed.

Before writing anything else about the seal, St. Alphonsus (1696-1787) set down the initial rule that in matters of the sacramental seal it is not lawful to use probable opinions.[3] Otherwise a probable injury would be perpetrated against the penitent and confession would be rendered odious. This rule flows from the general principle that probable opinions cannot be followed if their use would jeopardize the indisputable rights of others. In the case at hand, the penitent possesses the indisputable right of not suffering injury as a result of his confession. The penitent has the right to expect one hundred per cent observance of the seal. Probabilism, therefore, is not applicable in these matters. This is true concerning not only doubts of law but also doubts of fact about the seal.[4] Consequently, if it is disputed whether the law of the seal extends to a certain matter, the benefit of the doubt must be given to the seal and to the penitent. Likewise, if it is not clear in the confessor's mind, for example, whether he learned some particular information in or outside of confession, or whether a penitent confessed it sacramentally or not, the confessor must observe sacramental secrecy concerning it. Otherwise he would be risking a possible offense against the seal and against the indisputable rights of the penitent. Such risks one must preclude by excluding the application of probabilism in this realm.

With these two warnings in mind, one may now return to the original question. What facts or information is the confessor obliged not to reveal under any circumstances without the penitent's permission? The answer is presented in the following pages.

---

[3] ". . . non est licitum uti opinione probabili in praejudicium juris certi quod alter possidet; poenitens autem possidet jus ne occasione suae confessionis ullum patiatur gravamen."—*De Sacramento Poenitentiae—Theologia Moralis* (Editio nova a P. Leonardi Gaudé edita, 4 vols., Romae: Typographia Vaticana, 1905-1912), Lib. VI, n. 633.

[4] "Idque valet sive in dubio iuris, seu cum inter theologos non satis convenit, utrum hoc vel illud, quod ex confessione haustum fuisse constat, sub sigillo cadat; sive in dubio facti, seu cum dubitatur utrum aliquid cognitum sit ex confessione an ex alio fonte, vel cum dubitatur an aliquid a poenitente dictum sit in ordine ad confessionem."—Conte a Coronata, *Institutiones Iuris Canonici,* IV, n. 2132, p. 624.

SINS OF THE PENITENT

All sins confessed by the penitent for the sake of absolution fall within the protection of the seal.[5] It is immaterial whether the sin is occult or already publicly known; whether it is objective and/or subjective; formal or merely material; real or putative.

Mortal sins cannot be revealed in any way—numerically, specifically, or generically. The same is not true regarding venial sins. While the confessor cannot reveal the species or number of venial sins, he would not violate the seal by saying, for example, that a certain penitent had nothing more than venial sin to confess. (Note that the previous sentence read "venial sin," not "venial sins.") By making such a statement, the confessor would be disclosing no more than if he were to mention that the penitent in question went to confession. A manifestation of at least venial sin is required of every penitent desirous of sacramental absolution. To imply, however, that a penitent had a number of venial sins or more serious venial sin to confess would constitute a violation of the seal.[6] Likewise, to reveal the kind of venial sin confessed, even in the case of the slightest venial sin, violates the seal. Examples will perhaps clarify these norms:

The seal forbids the confessor to reveal:

(a) the species of mortal sin confessed. E.g., "Peter Penitent confessed adultery."

---

[5] This does not mean that the disclosure of a sin confessed would violate the seal even though the identity of the penitent who confessed it were absolutely concealed. Rather, the seal forbids the revelation of a sin confessed whenever there is either certainty or danger that the identity of the penitent who confessed it will be discovered. Cf. *supra*, p. 16. However, for the confessor to speak of sins heard in confession could violate an Instruction of the Holy Office, even though there were no danger of revealing the identity of the penitent. Cf. Appendix II, p. 110.

[6] "Si dicat Titium confessum esse *aliqua* venialia, aliquas venialitates, iuxta nonnullos sigillum non violat. Sed contraria sententia verior est ideoque in praxi retinenda. Sane aliud est dicere: Titius confessus est *sua venialia*, et aliud est dicere: Titius confessus est *aliqua* venialia. In priore casu, peccatum potest esse etiam unum vel alterum dumtaxat; in altero, peccata sunt plura. In priore casu, ex modo loquendi, venialia opponuntur mortalibus, quae proinde exclusa manent; non item in alio casu."—Cappello, *Tractatus Canonico-Moralis de Sacramentis*, II, n. 599, p. 620.

(b) the number of mortal sins. E.g., "Peter Penitent had two mortal sins to confess."

(c) mortal sin in general. E.g., "Peter Penitent confessed grave sin."

(d) the species of venial sin confessed. E.g., "Peter Penitent had nothing else to confess than that he stole five cents."

(e) the plurality of venial sins. E.g., "Peter Penitent confessed a number of venial sins."

The seal does not forbid the confessor to reveal:

(a) venial sin in general. E.g., "Peter Penitent has never had anything more to confess than venial sin."[7]

In reading literature on the seal, one constantly finds the statement that future sins, when confessed, constitute matter for sacramental secrecy. By future sins are meant those which are intended but not yet executed.[8] Future sins are intimately connected with a sinful intention. In view of this connection, they fall under the seal whenever the sinful intention is confessed in a sacramental way. So long as the sinful intention remains, the penitent, of course, cannot be absolved. But the future sin none the less enjoys the protection of the seal. Obvious as this might appear to the

---

[7] Authors completely discourage the making of such statements, however. E.g., "*Practice* tamen ab his aliisve locutionibus abstinendum omnino."—*Loc. cit.* This seems also to be the mind of the Code, which excludes confessors from giving testimony in processes of beatification and canonization. Cf. c. 2027, § 2, 1°.

"In certis casibus etiam peccata venialia in genere indicata seu manifestata possunt esse materia directa sigilli, ut si confessarius dicat de aliquo poenitente venialia peccata vel solum venialia confiteri coram iis personis quibus notum est illum poenitentem plura mortalia commisisse; item si confessarius unum poenitentem laudet quod sola venialia habeat et ea huius laudationis adiuncta sint, ut videri possit instituta quaedam comparatio cum aliis eiusdem confessarii poenitentibus, et eorum graviora peccata haec laudatio revelet."—Conte a Coronata, *op. cit.,* IV, n. 2134, p. 626.

[8] "Nomine peccati *futuri* intelligitur peccatum adhuc opere seu effectu committendum; quod fit, quando aliquis fatetur malum aliquod propositum, sive ab eodem proposito cessaverit, dum confitetur, sive in eo adhuc perseveret, sive exsecutus sit illud ex parte, sive nondum exsequi inceperit."—Ballerini-Palmieri, *Opus Theologicum Morale,* V, tr. 10, sect. 5, cap. 3, n. 924.

present-day reader, the point was controverted at one time in the history of the seal's development.[9]

Merely material sins and even entirely putative sins constitute matter of the seal when told in confession. Whatever the penitent confesses as a sin is covered by sacramental secrecy even if there is no actual guilt involved.[10] "Where there is not matter for confession and absolution, there still remains the obligation of sacramental secrecy, if a penitent has submitted, though mistakenly, something for absolution."[11]

Public sins, no less than occult sins, fall under the seal. For the confessor to say that a certain public sinner confessed this or that notorious sin with great sorrow and amendment would seem to redound to the penitent's credit rather than discredit. Even in these circumstances, however, the seal demands silence. The revelation of sins would ordinarily work to the shame and discredit of the penitent; it is purely accidental that in this or that particular case the contrary obtains. The law must regard the ordinary or normal course of events, and not isolated deviations. If any exceptions were admitted, the law of the seal would lose much of its value.[12] Penitents would always fear that further

---

[9] "Quidam Doctores subtraxerunt ab obiecto inviolabilitatis sigilli *peccatum intentionis,* seu, ut aiunt, peccatum futurum.

"Dicunt nempe quod si quis manifestet confessario intentionem perpetrandi aliquod delictum, quin eam retractet in actu confessionis, tale delictum potest a confessario revelari, quia, cum in eo casu sacramentum sit invalidum ob dispositionis defectum, delictum illud non pertinet ad sacramentum, quinimmo ei contrariatur, nec ideo est unde sibi reclamet sigilli sacramentalis protectionem. Hanc speciosam opinionem defenderunt in medio aevo Alex. Halensis et quidam alii."—Doronzo, *De Poenitentia,* II, 768. Cf. also Kurtscheid, *A History of the Seal of Confession,* p. 139.

[10] "Unde obiter infero, non solum vera peccata: sed ea etiam, quae peccata non sunt, et a poenitente dicuntur, quia putabat esse peccata, manere sub sigillo."—De Lugo, *De Sacramento Poenitentiae,* disp. 23, sect. 3, n. 59.

[11] Davis, *Moral and Pastoral Theology,* III, 317.

[12] "Et habenda est ut causa principalis legis sigilli possibilitas et periculum injuriae in Sacramentum, illud odiosum reddendo, quod periculum et possibilitas, regulariter loquendo, semper adest, et legis in praesumptione periculi fundatae semper obligant, etsi hic et nunc quis videatur ob peculiares circumstantias ab ea praesumptione eximi posse."—P. Rota, *Enchiridion Confessarii et Judicis Ecclesiastici,* pars. 1, sect. 1, cap. 1, n. 5.

exceptions would be presumed without sufficient justification.[13] The confessor might erroneously believe that this or that sin confessed was already the object of public knowledge whereas it was actually occult. Furthermore, the confessor's revealing that a public sin was told in confession would serve to confirm the presence of subjective guilt.[14]

All sins, therefore, manifested in sacramental confession are embraced by the seal. Of course, if the confessor knows the penitent's sins from two sources, sacramental and extra-sacramental, he would not violate the seal by speaking of these sins on the basis of his extra-sacramental knowledge of them. Caution would be demanded, however, lest he speak of the sins with more certainty or accuracy because of his confessional knowledge, or add details known only from confession.

CIRCUMSTANCES OF SINS

Any and all details which the penitent discloses to the confessor in order to explain or clarify his confession are what the authors have in mind when they speak here about circumstances of sins. In some instances, the penitent is obliged to confess this or that circumstance in order to make an integral confession. This is true, for example, of those factors which change the species of grave sins. At other times, while it is not strictly necessary, yet, it is useful and beneficial for the penitent to mention certain details about the sins confessed. At still other times the penitent recounts details which, not in his mind, but objectively, are superfluous.

---

[13] "Quarta difficultas est de peccatis publicis, de quibus aliqui dicunt, posse revelari: ut, si de homicida publico vel meretrice dicat: Audivi eorum peccata homicidii, et luxuriae cum magnis poenitentiae signis, hoc enim magis laudat, quam infamat poenitentem. . . . Sed contraria sententia est communis . . . quia per accidens est, quod id resultet hic et nunc in laudem poenitentis: attendi autem debet ad id quod est per se, scilicet, ne possit umquam loqui confessarius de his, quae audivit, ne semel data exceptione, saepe loquatur sine causa sufficienti."—De Lugo, *De Sacramento Poenitentiae,* disp. 23, sect. 3, n. 61. Cf. also Suarez, *De Poenitentia,* disp. 33, sect. 3, n. 6.

[14] "Revelatio peccati etiam notorii confessionem odiosam reddit; poenitentes enim facile timerent ne confessarius pro notorio habeat quod non est; et quia revelatione confessarii peccatum magis notorium et certum redderetur." —Regatillo, *Ius Sacramentarium,* n. 552, p. 320.

These details or circumstances, whether declared necessarily, advantageously, or superfluously, prudently or imprudently, generally fall under the seal if they are related by the penitent in order to explain or clarify the accusation of his sins. Otherwise the penitent would be deprived of that security and safeguard which is his due; confession would become odious and difficult for the faithful who, in many cases, are unable to distinguish between necessary and superfluous details. Just as the seal guards not only real but also putative sins, so also does it conceal not only real but also putative circumstances of sins.[15]

In the preceding paragraph, it was stated that circumstances of sins generally fall under the seal. An exception is admitted by authors. If the details or circumstances are publicly known and are in themselves innocuous to the penitent, then they are not matter for sacramental secrecy unless their repetition by the confessor would cause suspicion about the sin confessed. The example usually given of such publicly known and innocuous facts is the status of the penitent, e.g., whether he is a religious, a priest, a married person, etc.

> . . . object of the seal is everything said by the penitent that is intended to explain sins, whether it be useful, necessary, or unnecessary, unless the circumstances are matter of public knowledge though at the same time unknown to the confessor. Thus, the circumstances of a sin, such as occasions, motive, place, time, are objects of the seal, but publicly known circumstances, as that a penitent is married, are not *per se* objects of the seal, though they may accidentally be so.[16]

---

[15] "Infero secundo, non solum pertinere ad hoc sigillum illa, quae necessaria sunt omnino, sed etiam ea, quae utilia sunt, vel certe a poenitente aestimantur utilia ad melius declarandum suum peccatum . . . quia alioquin onerosa redderetur confessio, cum poenitens non sciat frequenter discernere, quae sint necessaria, quae utilia, quae inutilia ad eum finem."—De Lugo, *op. cit.*, disp 23, sect. 3, n. 59.

[16] Davis, *op. cit.*, III, 322. "Conditio, status poenitentis, v.g., num sit sacerdos, parochus, coniugatus, solutus, etc., per accidens possunt aliquando, etsi raro, cadere sub sigillum. Unde si confessarius diceret se id audivisse ex confessione et quidem in iis adiunctis quae audientibus suspicionem ingererent, poenitentem suam conditionem vel statum manifestasse ad aliquod peccatum declarandum, profecto laederet indirecte sigillum. Per se

A norm which several authors offer for use in the determining of which circumstances of sins fall under the seal is this: *sub sigillum cadunt illae peccatorum circumstantiae quas taceri poenitentis interest.*[17] However, the only category of circumstances which authors point out as not demanding sacramental secrecy are publicly known facts, such as the status attaching to one as married, as single, as a priest, as a religious, etc., the revelation of which would neither disclose the sin confessed nor otherwise aggrieve the penitent.

OBJECTS OF SINS

The object of a sin confessed constitutes material of the sacramental seal. What the authors mean here by objects of sins is best explained by the examples used by them. St. Alphonsus furnished two examples which are utilized by many modern authors: if a penitent confesses that he fostered hatred towards his mother because she was guilty of adultery, or that he failed to correct his brother who had committed a theft, the adultery of the mother and the theft of the brother would fall under the seal as objects of the sins confessed.[18] Ballerini (1805-1881)-Palmieri (1829-1909) added these further examples: If a penitent confessed that he needlessly revealed this or that occult crime of another, or that he despised his wife because of her infidelity, the occult crime and the infidelity would demand sacramental secrecy.[19]

Again, authors generally admit one exception. If the object of the penitent's sin is a publicly known fact, although previously unknown to the confessor, it would not demand the secrecy of the seal. For example, if a penitent confessed that he rejoiced at

---

tamen conditio vel status poenitentis, cum sint publica, sigillo non subsunt, quamvis lateant confessarium. Aliter dicendum si essent occulta."—Cappello, *Tractatus Canonico-Moralis de Sacramentis,* II, n. 601, p. 622.

[17] "Sunt generatim considerandae materia sigilli illae circumstantiae a poenitente in confessione manifestatae, quarum manifestatio extra confessionem gravamen aliquod afferret poenitenti, seu illae circumstantiae sunt materia sigilli quas taceri poenitentis interest."—Conte a Coronata, *Institutiones Iuris Canonici,* IV, n. 2137, pp. 627-628.

[18] *De Sacramento Poenitentiae,* cap. 3, dub. 1, n. 641.

[19] *Opus Theologicum Morale,* V, tr. 10, sect. 5, cap. 3, n. 947.

hearing that the mayor had been assassinated while reviewing a parade on a crowded street, the fact of the mayor's assassination would not fall under the seal, even though the confessor was previously unaware of the happening.[20] This presupposes, of course, that the confessor, by speaking about the assassination, would engender no suspicion about the sin of the penitent.[21]

ACCOMPLICE IN SIN

In making his confession, a penitent may possibly implicate an accomplice in his sins. He may confess, for example, that he and his brother stole something. If, as a consequence, the confessor realizes the name and sin of the accomplice, he is bound by sacramental secrecy concerning them. The penitent's imprudence in disclosing his accomplice does not diminish the confessor's obligation to observe silence. "The name and sin of an accomplice in sin, even if confessed without necessity, are matter of the seal, but the penitent may give permission to the confessor to use the knowledge so as to correct or warn another, a permission that should rarely be asked or used."[22]

PENANCE

The penance imposed cannot be revealed unless it is minimal. Otherwise a disclosure of the penance could easily arouse suspicions concerning the gravity of the number of sins confessed. Just as the confessor, without violating the seal, can say that a certain

---

[20] Cf. P. Rota, *op. cit.*, pars. 1, sect. 1, cap. 3, n. 19; Noldin-Schmitt, *Summa Theologiae Moralis* (Editio XXVII, 3 vols., Barcelona: Herder, 1951), III, n. 413, pp. 425-426.

[21] "Attamen censetur poenitens, si objectum sui peccati factum publicum et communiter notum erat, quamquam confessario forte ignotum, illius publici facti notitiam potius supponere vel praevie dare, quam sigillo claudere velle. Quod si constat, confessarius hanc notitiam non tenetur sub sigillo sacramentali secretam tenere. periculum tamen esse potest, si confessarius dicat, se ex confessione hanc notitiam habere."—Lehmkuhl, *Theologia Moralis* (Editio decima, 2 vols., Friburgi Brisgoviae: Sumptibus Herder, 1902), II, n. 459, p. 331.

[22] Davis, *Moral and Pastoral Theology,* III, 322-323. Cf. also, Ballerini-Palmieri, *op. cit.*, V, n. 926.

penitent confessed venial sin, but cannot say that the penitent confessed a number of venial sins, or more serious venial sins, or mortal sin, so also he can reveal a penance which points solely to venial sin, but not a penance which could suggest that a number of venial sins, or a more serious venial sin, or a mortal sin had been confessed.

ABSOLUTION

For the confessor to reveal that he granted sacramental absolution to a certain penitent would not in itself violate the seal. Such a statement, however, would indirectly violate the seal if it implied or aroused suspicions that others were not absolved. In practice, when asked, for example, by relatives, whether a particular person has received absolution, the confessor should always direct the inquirer to the penitent himself for an answer, explaining that such questions should not be asked of the confessor.

To reveal that absolution was either deferred or denied constitutes an infraction of the seal. This is true even in the case of a public sinner who openly declares to others that he was refused absolution.[23]

NATURAL DEFECTS

By natural defects, as distinguished from moral defects, are here meant a wide range of physical, mental, psychological, social, or other liabilities, such as illegitimacy of birth, deafness, timidity, disease, verbosity, low intelligence quotient, and so forth. During confession, one or another natural defect of the penitent might become evident to the confessor. Would he be bound by the seal not to disclose the defect in question?

In instances where the defect is actually related by the penitent for the purpose of explaining his sins, it is beyond all question that the confessor is bound by the seal not to reveal it. This is true even if the penitent was not obliged to mention the defect. As long as the penitent disclosed it for the purpose of clarifying his confession, it is matter of sacramental secrecy. If, for example, a

[23] Cf. Cappello, *op. cit.,* II, n. 601, pp. 621-622.

penitent confessed that he used the Lord's name in vain because of the vehement anger which overcame him when he discovered that he was an illegitimate child, the fact of the penitent's illegitimacy would demand sacramental secrecy.[24]

At other times the confessor's awareness of the penitent's natural defects is not based on the fact that the penitent reveals this or that defect for the sake of clarifying his self-accusation of sins. The confessor becomes aware of the defect *during confession* but not because it was disclosed by the penitent as a circumstance pertaining to the sins confessed. For instance, the confessor's awareness of the penitent's natural defects might come from the latter's actions or manner of confessing. Authors are not in agreement whether the seal would then oblige.

Some contend that such defects in no way pertain to the accusation of one's sins and, consequently, are not referable to the material of confession. They are not known by the priest as a result of anything the penitent revealed in confessing his sins. Rather, the priest sees or apprehends them for himself. Therefore they do not fall under the seal, but could constitute material for natural secrecy.[25]

Others disagree. They argue that the confessor learns these defects on the occasion of confession while the penitent is explaining his sins. For the confessor to speak about them to others would make the sacrament to some extent odious and would discourage the faithful from making their confessions. These defects, therefore, also fall under the seal. An exception obtains only then

---

[24] "Si confessarius tales defectus noverit, quatenus a poenitente fuerint manifestati ad explicanda peccata, tunc certe cadunt sub sigillo."—St. Alphonsus, *Theologia Moralis,* Lib. VI, n. 642.

[25] "Ratio autem est: quia defectus alii manifestantur a poenitente ad declarandum suam conscientiam, et peccata, et hi continentur sub sigillo. Alii fiunt ibi ab ipso poenitente, quos confessarius non audit ex relatione poenitentis; sed ipse eos videt et percipit: et hi, sicut non dicuntur secreto, sic non sunt sub sigillo. Nam, si poenitens sit blaesus, si rudis, si hebetis ingenii, qui, et similes defectus in confessione percipiuntur; non manent illi sub sigillo. Similiter ergo, si ostendit se naturae molestae, irresolutae, durioris ad credendum, qui omnes defectus ibi fiunt, et per consequens non sunt materia confessionis illius, non erunt sub sigillo."—De Lugo, *De Sacramento Poenitentiae,* disp. 23, sect. 3, n. 60.

when the confessor's speaking about them would in no wise be detrimental to the penitent.[26]

> What is to be said of the physical or mental defects which, in one way or another, come to the attention of the confessor during the course of the confession? Natural deficiencies must be considered matter of the seal either if they are manifested in order to explain some sin or if they are secret defects. Even though these latter are not mentioned by the penitent but are accidentally learned by the confessor, the priest must maintain sacramental secrecy in their regard.[27]

> The accidental object of the seal is any defect of the penitent observed during confession. . . . Such are . . . hidden defects mentioned in order to explain a sin, and such defects, though not so manifested, the revelation of which would offend a penitent, but not those which are publicly known, such as a penitent's deafness.[28]

Neither opinion holds that publicly known natural defects, such as the penitent's patent deafness, demand the secrecy of the seal.

Cappello gives a concise summary of both opinions and goes on to state his own view:

> Defectus *occulti,* si manifestentur *unice* ad peccatum declarandum, certe sunt materia sigilli.
>
> Si non manifestentur in hunc finem, sed *ex ipso modo confitendi* colligantur, controvertitur. Quidem censent cadere sub sigillum, tum quia ex *sola* confessione ac proinde scientia sacramentali cognoscuntur, tum quia revelatio huiusmodi defectum redderet odiosam confessionem.

---

[26] "Ratio, quia, cum defectus illi sunt odiosi, et confessarius noverit eos occasione confessionis dum poenitens sua peccata explicabat, eorum manifestatio semper redderet aliquo modo confessionem odiosam et ab ea retardaret. Tantummodo [contraria] sententia locum habere posset, quando omnino constaret confessario, poenitentem ex illius defectus manifestatione minime gravari."—St. Alphonsus, *op. cit.,* Lib. VI, n. 643.

"Defectus naturales materia sigilli sunt, non solum ubi ad explicandum peccatum dicuntur, sed etiam si ex sola confessione cognoscuntur, alias autem ignoti sunt."—Noldin-Schmitt, *Summa Theologiae Moralis,* III, n. 414, p. 426.

[27] Healy, "The Seal of Confession," *Review for Religious,* II (1943), 178.

[28] Davis, *Moral and Pastoral Theology,* III, 323.

> Alii dicunt non esse materiam sigilli, cum non manifestentur a poenitente *ad confitenda peccata sua,* nec ideo sacramentali scientia noscantur. Unde affirmant confessarium non laedere sigillum, si dicat poenitentem esse meticulosam, prolixum, nugis tempus terere, etc.
>
> Neutra sententia absolute et simpliciter admittenda videtur. Quare sic rectius distinguendum est: defectus *occulti,* quorum *manifestatio* inferret poenitenti *gravamen* —v.g. quod sit meticulosus—constituunt materiam sigilli; defectus *occulti,* e contra, quorum revocatio gravamen poenitenti non induceret, sigillo non subiacent.
>
> Practice vero omnes DD. admittunt tales defectus saltem sub secretum naturale cadere.
>
> Defectus *publici* sive *notorii,* v.g. surditas, coecitas, lingua impedita, etc., non sunt obiectum sigilli, quia, si confessarius de iis loquatur, poenitens id aegre ferre non potest.[29]

The writer prefers the first opinion. Defects which the penitent does not relate to the confessor but which the confessor himself notices from the penitent's manner of confessing are indeed apprehended on the occasion of confession. Furthermore, their revelation to others would undoubtedly be odious to the penitent. But they are not a part of the penitent's self-accusation. If the self-accusation is merely the occasion on which the confessor notices certain natural defects, this does not seem sufficient to verify the notion that the seal, and, consequently, the determination of its objects, presuppose and spring from sacramental confession, that is, from the penitent's self-accusation. Sacramental confession is the root or source of the seal; it is a cause, as it were, and not merely an occasion. In the case at hand, however, the penitent's self-accusation is merely the occasion on which the confessor notices certain natural defects in the penitent.[30]

---

[29] *Tractatus Canonico-Moralis de Sacramentis,* II, n. 604, p. 624.

[30] ". . . defectus illos confessarius non audit ex relatione poenitentis, sed ipse videt, et, sicut non dicuntur secreto, sic non sunt sub sigillo. Nec valet dicere quod hi defectus sint odiosi, et eos confessarius novit occasione confessionis; nam quis sanae mentis dixerit confessarium fregisse sigillum, si asseruerit se vidisse Titium, dum confiteretur, indutum caligis ac vestibus disruptis? Hoc, licet fortasse odiosum poenitenti quam maxime esse possit, et illicitum etiam aliquando dici queat, numquam tamen est manifestatio

SCRUPLES AND SCRUPULOSITY

If the priest knows from confession that a penitent is scrupulous, is he bound by the seal not to speak of this fact? Lehmkuhl (1834-1918) pointed out that such a question can be understood in four ways and, as a consequence, there are four answers:[31]

(a) Scruples which are confessed as sins are, as it were, putative sins. They fall under the seal just as much as real sins. All authors agree on this point.

(b) Scrupulosity which is related by the penitent as a circumstance of a sin confessed also falls under the seal in accordance with the norms already treated regarding circumstances of sins. For example, the penitent might confess that he was not sufficiently obedient to his director's instructions in fighting his scrupulosity. The fact of the penitent's scrupulosity would merit sacramental secrecy.

(c) To say that a penitent confessed many scruples would, in Lehmkuhl's opinion, violate the seal. It would amount to saying that the penitent had a number of sins to confess, albeit putative ones.[32]

(d) Finally, Lehmkuhl pointed out that at times scrupulosity is detected from the penitent's manner of speaking, of answering questions, etc. It is not disclosed by the penitent nor is it deduced from the contents of the penitent's self-accusation. Rather, it is perceived by the confessor from the penitent's mannerisms. Many authors hold that such scrupulosity detected from the penitent's manner of confessing does not fall under the seal; others disagree. The reasons for the difference of opinions are the same as those

---

sigilli, quia haec, nec a poenitente ipso, nec in ordine ad confessionem exponuntur."—P. Rota, *Enchiridion Confessarii et Judicis Ecclesiastici,* pars. 1, sect. 1, cap. 3, n. 25.

[31] Cf. Lehmkuhl, *Theologia Moralis,* II, n. 460, p. 332.

[32] Cf. *loc. cit.* "Scrupulositas poenitentis est certo objectum sigilli . . . cum innotescit confessario ex eo quod poenitens falso aut scrupuloso judicio deceptus multa confitetur uti peccati, quae talia non sunt."—Sabetti-Barrett, *Compendium Theologiae Moralis* (27 ed., New York: Pustet, 1919), n. 816, p. 791.

previously discussed under the treatment of those natural defects which are not revealed by the penitent but detected by the confessor from the penitent's mannerisms.[33]

IMPERFECTIONS

Included under the seal are those imperfections which the penitent either confesses as sins or else manifests in order to clarify the accusation of his sins.[34]

VIRTUES

The penitent's virtues as well as any other divine gifts constitute material of the seal if they were revealed by the penitent for a clearer explanation of his sins. Otherwise they are not objects of the seal, but could be protected by natural secrecy.[35] In processes of beatification and canonization, confessors are excluded from giving testimony concerning all things learned from or on the occasion of sacramental confession.[36]

---

[33] Cf. *supra*, p. 35. "Et quamvis probabile vel probabilius sit non esse materiam sigilli scrupulos qui a poenitente non declarantur ad manifestandam suam conscientiam, sed percipiuntur a confessario, attamen iam dictum est . . . in hac materia non licere uti opinione probabili."—Ferreres, *Compendium Theologiae Moralis* (17 ed., 10 post Codicem, quam recognovit A. Mondria, 2 vols., Barcinone: E. Subirana, 1949-1950), II, n. 711, p. 453.

[34] Cf. Cappello, *Tractatus Canonico-Moralis de Sacramentis,* II, n. 604, p. 624.

[35] "Hinc infero primo, quid dicendum sit de virtutibus, de revelationibus, et similibus gratiis, quas in confessione poenitens manifestat; de quibus universaliter dicunt aliqui, non esse materiam sigilli, cum non sint peccata, nec materia confessionis. . . . Sed distinguendum credo, aliquando enim praedicta dicuntur ad habendam instructionem a confessario, vel ad manifestandum integre conscientiae statum, et tunc non pertinent ad materiam confessionis, nec pertinent ad sigillum, sed ad secretum naturale. Aliquando vero dici possunt ad declarandum melius aliquod peccatum, v. gr. ingratitudinem erga Deum post haec et illa dona et beneficia Dei, vel inconstantiam in bono post tale propositum firmum procurandae perfectionis, et similia, et tunc credo quod pertineant ad sigillum."—De Lugo, *De Sacramento Poenitentiae,* disp. 23, sect. 3, n. 58; cf. also, St. Alphonsus, *Theologia Moralis,* Lib. VI, n. 641.

[36] Cf. cc. 2027, § 2, 1°, and 1757, § 3, 2°.

ADVICE

Advice sought in confession is protected by the seal when it is related to the penitent's confession. This would be verified, for example, if the penitent were to ask the confessor to suggest some remedy for this or that sin disclosed in confession, or to advise him on the best way to avoid some occasion of sin. "Advice asked a confessor will be an object of the seal if the request has any bearing on sins confessed; otherwise it is not."[37]

SINS COMMITTED DURING CONFESSION

It could happen that a penitent would commit a sin during confession. He might, for example, lose his temper or insult the confessor. Such actions on the penitent's part constitute material of the seal only if they are subsequently confessed as sins. The confessor could not speak of them in any case, however, if his doing so would arouse suspicions about the confession. To say, for instance, that a certain penitent became angry in confession might easily suggest that absolution had been denied or that some serious matter was involved.

> Sins committed during confession, as impatience with and disobedience to the confessor, if accused as sins, are matter of the seal, otherwise they are not, unless their revelation might give ground to others for suspicion of a penitent's other sins.
>
> Theft committed during the course of confession and not confessed is not matter of the seal; and if a confession clearly appeared to be only a pretext for finding an opportunity of theft from the confessor, it is not a sincere confession and would not be matter of the seal.[38]

FACT OF CONFESSION

For the confessor to state that a given person made his confession would not in itself violate the seal. However, if such a statement, in view of particular circumstances, would raise suspi-

[37] Davis, *Moral and Pastoral Theology*, III, 322.

[38] Davis, *op. cit.*, III, 323.

cions about the need of the confession in question, then, according to many authors, the seal forbids the confessor to disclose the fact of confession.

> That one comes to confession is of itself a public fact to which the confessor is a witness. Hence, it is not matter of the seal. . . . If, however, a man approaches a priest in secret to go to confession, his coming to the Sacrament is not public but secret. Since knowledge of this secret fact could easily give rise to suspicion of serious sin, it becomes matter of the seal.[39]

IMPERTINENT STATEMENTS

Statements or disclosures made by the penitent in the confessional or on the occasion of confession but entirely irrelevant to the actual confession obviously do not fall under the seal.

> Though the subject-matter of the seal is very extensive, there is, nevertheless, certain knowledge acquired in sacramental confession which does not fall under the seal. In this category belong statements made clearly by way of digression which in no way pertain to the sins submitted to the Power of the Keys. An example of this is the remark: "Father, my new home is finished now. Will you bless it when you have time?" The knowledge thus imparted is given extra-sacramentally.[40]

SINS IN A COMMUNITY

By "community" is intended any group of persons united in one way or another under a common name, such as a city, a town, a parish, a high school class, a religious house, and the like. By "sins in a community" are here meant the sins confessed by one or several members of the group, which, when revealed, are predicated of the community rather than of the individual. Is it

---

[39] Healy, "The Seal of Confession," *Review for Religious*, II (1943), 178. Cf. also Conte a Coronata, *Institutiones Iuris Canonici*, IV, n. 2140, p. 630. According to Conte a Coronata, others disagree with the assertion that the fact of confession falls under the seal if its disclosure would cause suspicions about the accusation of mortal sin. Rather, it would be the object of natural secrecy. Cf. *ibid.*, footnote 1.

[40] Healy, "art. cit.," *Review for Religious*, II (1943), 178.

contrary to the seal for a confessor, *using his sacramental knowledge,* to reveal that such and such a grave sin has been committed in a particular community? Examples: "Many people in this parish are missing Mass on Sunday." "In my conference today I want to talk about obedience, because I know that one or two members in this religious house need some help in this regard." "In spite of their Catholic education, one or two members of the sophomore class haven't learned the futility of making sacrilegious confessions." What are the possible results of such disclosures in the minds of third parties (i.e., parties other than the penitent)?

(a) The listener in some circumstances may very well suspect the actual person or persons about whom the confessor is speaking. If so, the confessor's statement amounts to or at least causes danger of a revelation of both sin and penitent. His statement in such instances is manifestly against the seal, because it adds up to an indirect betrayal of the sinner (*proditio peccatoris*).

(b) At other times, the listener may in no way suspect the identity of the penitent or penitents referred to by the confessor. However, if the community in question is not somewhat large, such disclosures by the priest bring a certain amount of shame, embarrassment, or diminution of good name to the whole community, to all the members of the community, and, consequently, to the penitent himself. While the confessor cannot be charged with betraying the identity of the sinner and his sin (*proditio peccatoris*), nevertheless he is guilty of revealing something from confession which is offensive and harmful to the penitent. This is contrary to the seal as it derives from the divine law.[41]

[41] "Et sane Doctores quaestionem generalem instituere consueverunt, an contra sigillum foret manifestare peccata alicuius loci aut cuiuspiam coetus. . . . Quaestionem generaliter propositam, generalibus quoque principiis resolvebant, statuentes, nunc peccari etiam contra sigilli legem, quando ex huiusmodi revelatione vel 1° ansa daretur suspicandi de personis particularibus, vel 2° infamia redundaret in illam communitatem sive loci sive coetus, quae infamia recidit in ipsum poenitentem, quatenus membrum communitatis necessario particeps est infamiae totius corporis, cuius pars est atque adeo merito haec revelatio cedere in gravamen ipsius quoque poenitentis et confessio fieri exosa et odiosa; exosum enim poenitenti est, quod e sua confessione ansa sumitur adspergendi illam infamiam etc."—Ballerini-Palmieri, *Opus Theologicum Morale,* V, n. 994.

A number of authors consider communities of less than 3,000 persons as sufficiently small to suffer detriment from the confessor's revealing defamatory sins which occurred there.[42] Aertnys (1825-1915)-Damen (1881-1953) held the same figure, but they specified that defamation of the community results from the disclosure of *occult* sins.[43] Wouters (1864-1933) increased the number to 6,000 or 7,000 and intended a particularly defamatory sin, such as sodomy or bestiality; he pointed out that this figure refers to the number of Catholics in a particular locality.[44] Vermeersch seemed to imply an obsolescence for the figure 3,000.[45] In any case, certainly small groups, such as a particular religious house or a particular high school class, could easily feel injured, and justly so, if the confessor were to disclose the serious sins of one or several unidentified members of the group.

Vermeersch explained that the resulting injury to the community and, consequently, to the penitent, depends also on the quality of the person to whom the confessor makes the disclosure:

> Interdum qualitas personae *cui res dicitur efficiet ut facta communicatio sit paenitenti onerosa et ingrata vel non.* Supponimus semper nullam criminis seu peccati suspicionem in ipsum paenitentem cadere.
>
> Etenim alii aliis facilius mirantur talia vel talia accidisse; vel levius, propter culpam paucorum, multos suspectos habent. Hominum experientia seniorem confessarium docebit nullatenus minoris aestimare clerum

---

[42] Cf., e.g., Fanfani, *Manuale Theoretico-Practicum Theologiae Moralis* (4 vols., Romae: Libraria "Ferrari," 1950-1951), IV, n. 428, p. 553; Prümmer, *Manuale Theologiae Moralis* (Editio decima recognita ab E. M. Münch, 3 vols., Barcelona: Herder, 1945-1946), III, n. 447, p. 320.

[43] Cf. *Theologia Moralis* (Editio XVI, VIII post codicem, 2 vols., Torino: Marietti, 1950), II, n. 465, p. 347.

[44] Cf. *Manuale Theologiae Moralis,* II, n. 438, p. 344.

[45] "Quod ad loci diffamationem: hodie in pluribus regionibus tanta est diversitas religionis et morum, seu opinandi et agendi, ut proprio veluti nomine seu fama carere videatur, ita ut *unius* scelus, etiam enorme, certeros incolas nullatenus inficiat.

"*Magis tamen probrosum erit,* si dicas, vitium occultum, morbum venereum ibidem dominari. Olim, sub hoc respectu distinguebant a maioribus locis ea quae minus quam tria milia incolarum numerabant."—*Theologia Moralis,* III, n. 474, p. 303.

> vel monasterium eo quod non nulli libidinosos actus fecerint, dum, contra, id rescire non parum nocebit famae sacerdotum vel religiosorum apud *laicum* qui haec in sanctuario accidere posse, ne suspicabatur quidem. Si duo confessarii qui *simul* excipiunt confessiones *eiusdem partis* cleri, ita ut idem genus hominum audierint, alter alteri iudicium suum de morali eorum condicione communicent, neuter ad alterius scientiam quidpiam addet, ita ut sermo iste, numquam sane suadendus, ab omni sigilli violatione immunis esse possit; contra, existimationem istius cleri minueret idem sermo habitus apud eos qui paenitentes istos non audiverint.[46]

Finally, Vermeersch advised pastors and confessors not to employ their confessional knowledge in pointing out to preachers those vices which need particular attention, as, for example, during the time of a mission.[47]

In concluding this section, one should point out that even if the confessor in certain instances does not cause (a) or (b) explained above, nevertheless, by speaking of the sins in a community, he may very well be violating the directions of the Holy Office regarding this matter.[48] Furthermore, if the penitent himself realizes that the confessor is speaking of his confession, the confessor would be guilty of confronting the penitent with the sins he confessed, an illicit action to be treated in a later chapter.[49]

SINS WITHOUT REFERENCE TO PENITENT

If a confessor, keeping silence about anything that might in any way identify the person of the penitent, were to disclose in private conversation or in public sermons matter revealed to him in confession, he would not be guilty of violating the substance of the sacramental seal. To the faithful, however, his conversation could appear to violate sacramental secrecy; his action could cause the faithful to suspect and fear a lack of complete observance of the seal. By diminishing their confidence in the protection of the

---

[46] *Ibid.*, n. 473, pp. 302-303.
[47] Cf. *ibid.*, n. 474, p. 303.
[48] Cf. Appendix II, p. 110.
[49] Cf. *infra*, p. 77.

seal, he would make confession more difficult for them. Thus, while not substantially violating the seal, he would none the less be causing what the seal is intended to prevent. An Instruction of the Holy Office issued in 1915 completely forbade the confessor to mention in public or private talks anything pertaining to the matter of sacramental confession, except in the case of necessary consultation.[50]

Even prior to 1915, authors repeatedly issued the same warning both because of the scandal involved for the faithful and because of the danger of causing unsuspected revelations of confession.[51]

CONCLUSION TO CHAPTER

The preceding pages of this chapter have answered the initial question: What facts or information is the confessor obliged not to reveal under any circumstances without the penitent's permission? In Chapter II, the meaning of the seal as defined in canon 889, that is, the *non-proditio peccatoris,* was examined. It is the obligation not to reveal in a conjoint manner the sinner and his sin. From a comparison of Chapter III with Chapter II it appears that authors, in investigating and determining the matter

---

[50] The full text of the Instruction is given in Appendix II, cf. *infra,* p. 110. "Even with regard to virtues it would be clearly contrary to the instruction of the Holy Office to refer our knowledge to confession, for example, by saying: 'you can tell from his confession that he's an angel.' "—Kelly, *The Good Confessor* (New York: Sentinel Press, 1951), p. 46.

[51] E.g., "Nulla est sigilli violatio si quis narret peccatum in confessione auditum, ita ut nullo indicio revelari possint peccatores. Attamen, seclusa utilitate instructionis vel consilii petendi, a similibus narrationibus generatim abstinendum est; ratio, quia audientes laici, praesertim simplices, facile scandalizantur, suspicantes violari sigillum. Et quandoque in frequentibus et promiscuis istis colloquiis periculum est, ne in suspicionem poenitentibus quis inducatur, imo et sequatur revelatio."—Gury, *Compendium Theologiae Moralis,* II, n. 664, pp. 639-640.

"Non solum cum aliis, clericis vel laicis, colloquendo, sed etiam concionando dum vitia reprehendit, quâ maxima potest sollicitudine caveat [Sacerdos], ne locus adsit suspicandi, ipsum scientiâ ex sacramenti hujus administratione hausta abuti. Id enim jure merito haud parum scandali apud auditores parit, verbum Dei ludibrio exponit, et ipsum Sacramentum reddit odiosum."—*Concilii Plenarii Baltimorensis II Acta et Decreta* (Baltimorae: Excudebat Joannes Murphy, 1868), decr. 290.

protected by the seal against revelation, used a broader yardstick than the canonical seal's ***non-proditio peccatoris***. Rather, they used some such a principle as this: The confessor can under no circumstances reveal either the sinner and his sin, or anything else disclosed to the confessor by the penitent, the *revelation* of which would be displeasing and odious to penitents.

An example will serve to illustrate the need for this broader yardstick. The confessor is not allowed to reveal the occult object of a sin. E.g., Simon Sinner confesses that he hated his mother because he discovered that she was guilty of adultery. The object of Simon's sin includes the adultery of his mother. If, by revealing that Mrs. Sinner committed adultery, the confessor would arouse suspicion about Simon's sin, then, of course, the revelation would constitute the *proditio peccatoris* of canon 889. But if the disclosure would in no way point to Simon and to his sin, it would not betray Simon, the penitent, in the technical sense of *proditio peccatoris*. Nevertheless, the disclosure even in this second hypothesis would never be lawful without Simon's permission. The publication of his mother's sin of adultery presumably would be offensive to and contrary to the wishes of Simon even though it in no way indicated his own sin. The fact of his mother's adultery is obnoxious to Simon both in itself and in its relation to his own sin. Simon, therefore, has the inviolable right to protection against disclosure of the fact, not only in its relation to his own sin but also in itself. But only if his mother's infidelity would in some way be referable to his own sin would the disclosure, in the writer's opinion, violate the law enjoined in canon 889. Authors generally do not seem to make this distinction but the writer believes it is necessary to do so.

The need for the broader yardstick is verified also by the fact that when a penitent, while confessing his own sins, identifies an accomplice in sin, the confessor is not at liberty to speak of the sin of the accomplice even if by doing so he would in no way cause danger of a betrayal of the penitent. Furthermore, the broader yardstick more easily explains why public and non-defamatory facts, such as the status of the penitent (e.g., a married person, a religious, a priest), do not in themselves call for sacramental secrecy even though they were mentioned by the penitent in order to clarify the accusation of his sins.

The IV General Council of the Lateran enunciated the basic obligation of sacramental secrecy—the *non-proditio peccatoris*—which has become the canonical definition of the seal. It was only after this Council that theologians really developed in detail the more intimate questions concerning sacramental secrecy, such as the full extent of the matter protected against revelation. While the theologians undoubtedly received impetus from the decree of the Lateran Council, the writer believes that, in determining the matter which falls under sacramental secrecy, they used a principle derived from the divine law that is broader than the *non-proditio peccatoris* which, as mentioned in the IV General Council of the Lateran, constitutes the definition of the canonical seal.

In the writer's opinion, the matter guarded by the divine seal against revelation will also fall into the sphere of the canonical seal to the extent that its revelation would cause the *proditio peccatoris*. Chrétien can profitably be quoted at length regarding the object or matter of what he calls the *"sigillum proprie dictum"* which corresponds to the "canonical seal" in the terminology of this dissertation:

> Principium. Materia sigilli constat iis omnibus confessione sacramentali cognitis quorum revelatio aliquatenus peccatorem prodere potest.—Hoc manifestum est ex verbis can. 889, § 1, et ex rationibus legis supra expositis.
>
> Duo proinde requiruntur et sufficiunt ut aliquid sit materia sigilli et sub lege cadat.
>
> A. Requiritur ut ea *sola confessione sacramentali cognita* sint. . . .
>
> B. Requiritur ut eorum revelatio *aliquatenus prodere possit poenitentem.* Iam vero talia sunt, non solum ea quae in iudicio poenitentis sunt materia confessionis, sed etiam ea quae cum aliqua etsi parva probabilitate ducere possunt in notitiam peccatorum alicuius poenitentis.
>
> a) *Peccata accusata* sunt materia propria sigilli, quia eorum revelatio natura sua prodit poenitentem. Sive sint mortalia etiam generaliter revelata sive venialia, sive effective commissa sive tantum proposita, sive vitae anteactae sive ab ultima confessione patrata, sive publica sive occulta, sive formalia sive subiectiva tantum vel

erronee ut peccata accusata, sunt certo obiectum sigilli. . . .

b) *Alia cum accusatione connexa,* item satis facile sunt materia sigilli, si et in quantum proditura sint poenitentem, in eo quod ad cognitionem ipsorum peccatorum determinati poenitentis ducere possint.

—Talia sunt:

1. quaedam *circumstantiae peccatis extrinsecae,* de se indifferentes sed de facto connexionem habentes cum peccato, quae declaratae sunt a poenitente ad pleniorem intelligentiam peccati, ita ut earum revelatio in aliorum mentibus suspicionem excitet de ipso peccato. Sic causa vel occasio peccati, v.g. adulterium matris quod fuit causa peccati odii, peccata complicis, conditio vel status poenitentis, quod sit illegitimus, caelebs, coniugatus, sacerdos, possunt esse materia sigilli et revelari nequeunt sine periculo prodendi poenitentem.

2. quidam *defectus* poenitentis, etsi de se non sint materia sigilli, de facto tamen connexionem cum peccato haberi possunt: sic, quamvis raro, defectus *naturales,* v.g. impatientia, hebetudo, vel defectus *morales,* ut scrupulositas, si v.g. revelentur scrupuli qui tanquam peccata accusati sunt.

3. *consilia petita* a poenitente et monitiones datae a confessario; haec enim alios facile ad suspicanda peccata ducunt.

4. *poenitentia imposita,* nisi sit minima, qualis pro levissimis peccatis imponi consuevit.

5. *absolutio negata,* etiamsi ipse poenitens hoc sit fassus, propter quod occasionem dat suspicandi gravia peccata commissa; immo *absolutio concessa,* si audientes, propter silentium de alio poenitente, hunc supponant gravis peccati reum.

6. *accessus ad confessionem* de se non est materia sigilli; extraordinariis tamen in circumstantiis potest eius cognitio pro superioribus, parentibus esse signum quod accedens graviter relapsus sit.[52]

---

[52] *De Sigillo Sacramentali,* pp. 105-106.

CHAPTER IV

SUBJECTS BOUND BY THE SEAL

Who is bound by the sacramental secrecy of the seal? The scope of this chapter is to present a summary of the answers given to this question by theologians and canonists. For the most part, the authors are in agreement concerning the answer, but some points are disputed.[1]

In this chapter, there is no need to distinguish between the divine seal and the canonical seal. The subjects bound by the seal are identical in both cases. The seal as derived from the divine law and the seal as defined in canon 889 oblige the same persons. The penalties established in the Code for violators of the seal vary for different subjects. But this question is the matter for a latter chapter.[2]

After declaring explicitly that both the confessor and the interpreter are obliged by the secrecy of the seal, canon 889 goes on to include under this obligation all others to whom confessional matter has become known in any manner whatsoever. The confessor, interpreter, and all others who receive confessional information are, therefore, subjects bound by the seal. Whether the knowledge is obtained immediately from the penitent's self-accusation or at second hand, lawfully or unlawfully, the recipient of it has the duty of preserving sacramental secrecy unless he be excused by the penitent.[3]

CONFESSOR

The confessor is the primary subject bound by the seal's obliga-

---

[1] The reader is again warned that probabilism cannot be used in resolving doubts concerning the seal. Furthermore, a subject not bound by the seal might none the less be bound by natural and committed secrecy regarding a matter in question.

[2] Cf. *infra*, Chapter VI, p. 84.

[3] Cf. Doronzo, *De Poenitentia*, II, 848.

tion. To him alone does the penitent reveal his sins *ut Deo.*[4] Does "confessor" here include priests who lack the necessary jurisdiction? Furthermore, does the term include laymen (or, for that matter, clerics who are not priests) erroneously considered by the penitent to be priests? Recall that sacramental confession alone gives rise to the obligation of the seal. One of the requisites for sacramental confession is that it be made to an authorized priest. To fulfill this requirement in matters of the seal, is it sufficient that the penitent is under the impression that the person to whom he confesses is an authorized priest? Is the subjective belief of the penitent sufficient, or must the requisite of confessing to an authorized priest be verified objectively? Authors disagree.

For the sake of clarity, the two cases will be treated separately, the case of confession to a layman being considered before the case of confession to a priest devoid of confessional faculties. Authors today are in agreement that confession to a layman, *known as such,* would not be sacramental and could not give rise to the obligation of the seal.[5] On the other hand, if confession is made to a layman believed by the penitent to be an authorized priest, would the fraudulent confessor in such a case be bound by the seal? There is no unanimity in the replies of the authors.

Some maintain that the seal is operative only if the elements of sacramental confession are objectively realized. (Immaterial to this issue is the fact of whether contrition, absolution, and satisfaction are present.) One of these elements is the confessor. A layman, even though considered by the penitent to be an authorized confessor, is not one objectively. In the opinion of these authors, the manifestation of sins to such a layman is not even an in-

---

[4] Cf. Cappello, *Tractatus Canonico-Moralis de Sacramentis,* II, n. 594, p. 612.

[5] "Certum est, imprimis *diaconos* audivisse saeculis elapsis confessionem; hanc diaconorum potestatem audiendi confessionem admissam fuisse a nonnullis sanctis Patribus eamque plura Concilia particularia recognovisse. . . . Item certum est confessionem, in casu necessitatis, institutam fuisse apud *laicos,* imo eam instituendam esse nonnulli DD. expresse docuerunt." —Cappello, *op. cit.,* II, n. 272, p. 235.

choatively sacramental act. Accordingly, it cannot give rise to the seal. Illustrative of this opinion are the words of Hürth-Abellan:

> Sigillum sacramentale supponit aliquem actum vere sacramentalem et non efficitur nisi per actum qui saltem inchoative fuerit sacramentalis. . . . Hinc sigillum non oritur: 1° ex sola voluntate poenitentis aut confessarii, quin obiective positus fuerit actus vere sacramentalis; 2° neque ex mera bona aut mala fide alterutrius. . . . Confessio facta laico (licet poenitens putet eum esse sacerdotem), nullo mode, ne inchoative quidem, est obiective sacramentalis.[6]

Admitting that fewer theologians hold this opinion, Kurtscheid (1877-1941) none the less believed that an objective examination of the question revealed no other obligation than that of natural silence. "The mistake or good faith of the penitent does not alter the fact that his confession in itself is not sacramental, because not made to a priest."[7] Likewise, Davis (1866-1952) wrote that "one not a priest who plays the fictitious role of confessor is probably not bound by the sacramental seal."[8] Cappello, too, holds this as the more probable opinion.[9]

A greater number of authors, however, include under the seal the layman who plays the role of a confessor. While it is true that all three elements in the notion of sacramental confession are not objectively realized when confession is made to a bogus priest, nevertheless some of them are, namely, the manifestation of sins by a penitent whose intention is to obtain sacramental absolution. In the minds of these authors, this is sufficient to engender the obligation of the seal even though the manifestation of sins is made to one who objectively is not a confessor. Since the purpose of the seal is to protect the penitent, it obliges if the

---

[6] *De Sacramentis* (Romae: Pont. Univ. Gregoriana, 1947), nn. 420-422, pp. 234-235. Cf. also D'Annibale, *Summula Theologiae Moralis* (Editio quinta, 3 vols., Romae: Desclée, Lefebvre et Soc., 1908), III, n. 357, pp. 304-305; Vermeersch, *Theologia Moralis,* III, n. 463, p. 298; Ferreres, *Compendium Theologiae Moralis,* II, n. 705, pp. 448-449.

[7] *A History of the Seal of Confession,* pp. 253-254.

[8] *Moral and Pastoral Theology,* III, 319.

[9] *Op. cit.,* II, n. 595, pp. 612-613.

penitent confesses in good faith to one erroneously believed to be a priest.[10]

Suarez (1548-1617) and De Lugo (1583-1660) present an interesting difficulty, the discussion of which by them may add some clarification to this second opinion.[11] Both of these authors agreed that confession made to a layman when known as such by the penitent does not furnish a foundation for the obligation of the seal. Suarez and De Lugo also maintained that confession made to a layman whom the penitent believes to be a priest does give rise to the obligation. Suppose that a person under the false impression that a layman could forgive sins were to confess his sins to such a lay person.[12] Would he not be confessing his sins for the sake of absolution and thereby be protected by the seal just as much as the person who confesses to a layman, if such a person believed the layman to be a priest? In each case there is a manifestation of sins, the intention of obtaining absolution, and an error. The answer given by Suarez and De Lugo was based on the difference between the errors in the two cases. In the instance of the penitent who unknowingly confessed to a layman, the error was one of fact—the fact that this person was a layman and not a priest. In the case of the one who believed that laymen can forgive sins, the error was one *in iure*. The error of fact did not prevent the penitent from knowing and intending the true confession and absolution

---

[10] "Cum enim sigillum sit in favorem poenitentis, obligatio sigilli oritur si ipse ex parte sui posuerit necessaria ad confessionem sacramentalem eamque ad absolutionem ordinaverit."—Merkelbach, *Summa Theologiae Moralis,* III, n. 623, p. 585.

"Sexto dubitatur de eo, qui se sacerdotem fingit, et audit confessionem, an obligetur ad sigillum sacramentalem: de quo etiam est ratio dubitandi, cum illa non sit confessio sacramentalis, ex qua sola sigillum oritur. . . . Communiter tamen omnes agnoscunt eamdem obligationem. . . . Ratio autem est: quia ex intentione, saltem poenitentis, fuit confessio sacramentalis, cum ipse ea intentione confessus sit, ut obtineat absolutionem a Christo institutam."—De Lugo, *De Sacramento Poenitentiae,* disp. 23, sect. 2, n. 40.

[11] Cf. Suarez, *De Poenitentia,* disp. 33, sect. 2, n. 3; De Lugo, *De Sacramento Poenitentiae,* disp. 23, sect. 2, nn. 41-42.

[12] "From the beginning of the 11th century we encounter the view that venial sins, and, in case of urgent necessity, also grievous sins, may be confessed to a layman."—Kurtscheid, *op. cit.,* p. 246.

established by Christ. The error or ignorance *in iure,* on the other hand, did preclude the person's intending the true sacrament instituted by Christ. He intended not Christ's institution, namely confession to a priest, but, rather, confession to a layman, which Christ did not establish. Christ imposed the obligation of the seal in favor of His sacrament, but not in favor of a fiction entirely different from it. The case of factual error differed, therefore, from the case of error *in iure.* In the former, the penitent *intended* to confess to a priest; in the latter, he *intended* to confess to a layman.

So much for the layman. There remains the question of the priest who hears confessions although devoid of confessional faculties. Is he bound by the seal?

In answering this question, Suarez pointed out three sets of possibilities:

(a) Both penitent and confessor are in good faith regarding the lack of necessary faculties.

(b) The penitent, but not the confessor, is in good faith.

(c) Both penitent and priest are aware of the deficiency.[13]

According to Suarez, the seal obliges whenever (a) or (b) are verified. The third set of circumstances, those under (c), calls for a further distinction. The confession could be made either with the hope of the priest's obtaining jurisdiction and, consequently, with a sacramental intent, or else without such a hope and intent. If made with the hope of the priest's obtaining jurisdiction, the confession was an inchoatively sacramental one, and the seal accordingly bound the priest. This was verified, for example, when a reserved sin was confessed to a priest lacking faculties to absolve from such a sin, in order that he might seek the necessary jurisdiction. On the other hand, if the penitent, without this intention of having the required faculties procured, manifested his sins to a priest known by him to lack jurisdiction, then the confession was in no way sacramental and did not give rise to the seal.

Other authors, without enunciating the distinctions made by Suarez, merely state that confession made to a priest who lacks confessional faculties begets the obligation of the seal if the

---

[13] Cf. *op. cit.,* disp. 33, sect. 2, n. 4.

penitent is unaware of the lack of faculties, but does not beget such an obligation if the penitent is aware of the deficiency.[14]

It could seem that those authors who contend that the seal does not bind a layman who poses as a confessor would draw the same conclusion regarding the priest who, unknown to the penitent, lacks jurisdiction. However, they maintain that there is no parity between the two cases, since the priest who hears confessions without faculties could immediately be granted the required jurisdiction. According to these authors, confession in good faith to a layman believed to be a priest is not objectively sacramental, not even inchoatively; but every confession made in good faith to a priest, even to one who lacks jurisdiction, for the purpose of absolution, is at least inchoatively sacramental.[15] "Every confessor who acts as confessor, whether or not he has faculties to absolve, even one who is excommunicated, suspended, or under interdict, or deprived of office, or degraded, is bound to inviolable secrecy."[16]

INTERPRETER

Canon 903 makes optional the use of an interpreter by those who cannot otherwise express their sins to the confessor. In all

[14] Conte a Coronata, for example, writes: "Sacramentalis est etiam confessio facta laico vel sacerdoti non confessario, qui confessarios se finxerint et tales reputentur a poenitente. E contra non esset sacramentalis confessio scienter facta laico vel sacerdoti iurisdictione carenti."—*Institutiones Iuris Canonici,* IV, n. 2129, p. 621.

[15] "Attamen iure censent omnem confessionem sacerdoti (licet hic iurisdictione hic et nunc careat) sincere factam in ordine ad absolutionem obtinendam dici posse et debere inchoative sacramentalem, cum cuilibet sacerdoti iurisdictio requisita ad valorem statim dari possit."—Hürth-Abellan, *op. cit.,* n. 422, p. 235.

"Non tamen videtur teneri *laicus* qui se fingeret confessarium et cui poenitens bona fide confiteretur. Nam talis confessio ne inchoative quidem est *obiective* sacramentalis. . . . Nec valet paritas cum sacerdoti *sine iurisdictione,* cui *statim* dari potest iurisdictio ad valorem necessaria."—Ferreres, *op. cit.,* II, n. 705, pp. 448-449.

"Verum procul dubio sub sigillum cadit quod accusatur sacerdoti carenti iurisdictione. Namque ut confessio compleatur absolutione valida, satis est ut minister ille iurisdictione muniatur."—Vermeersch, *op. cit.,* III, n. 463, p. 298.

[16] Davis, *op. cit.,* III, 319.

cases, abuse and scandal must be prevented, and canon 889, § 2, is to be observed. Canon 889, § 2, states explicitly that the interpreter is bound by the seal of confession. This means an interpreter used during the actual confession. Not included under the obligation of the seal is an interpreter who, before confession, coaches a penitent on the correct manner of expressing his sins.[17]

THE SUPERIOR IN RESERVED CASES

The Sacred Penitentiary, the local ordinary, or some other superior must be approached at times for faculties to grant absolution in reserved cases. Similarly, if absolution is conferred in such cases by virtue of the emergency powers granted in canons 2252 and 2254, subsequent recourse to the Penitentiary, local ordinary, or other superior is demanded. These superiors from whom faculties are requested, or to whom subsequent recourse is made, are bound by the seal of confession. This is true whether they are approached by the confessor or by the penitent himself, whether orally or in writing. The request for faculties is a necessary antecedent of absolution; the recourse after absolution is a required complement of it. In both cases the superior constitutes one sacramental tribunal with the confessor.[18]

> In most cases, of course, it will suffice to ask him [i.e., the superior] for the necessary faculty without mentioning any name. Should he, however, in spite of all

[17] "Interpres sigillo tenetur tantum, si in ipsa confessione adhibitus fuit; non si solum antea ad confessionem preparandam."—Regatillo, *Ius Sacramentarium,* n. 551, p. 319.

"Si poenitens *ante* confessionem usus fuerit interprete ut se apte ad illam pararet, hic sigillo sacramentali non tenetur. Sane requiritur, ut interpres adhibeatur *in ipso actu confessionis,* tanquam medio communicationis inter poenitentem et confessarium."—Cappello, *Tractatus Canonico-Moralis de Sacramentis,* II, n. 596, p. 615.

[18] "[Tenetur ad sigillum] Superior, ad quem sive poenitens sive confessarius . . . pro casu reservato similive causa recursum habuit *sive verbo sive per literas.* Videlicet ille Superior cum confessario ipso unum quoddam tribunal facit, ad quod poenitens pro confessione confugere *debet*: et quamquam per literas non semper confugere debet, eam viam eligere tamen iure suo potest. Quare in hoc casu literae datae vere ad notitiam sacramentaliter datam pertinent."—Lehmkuhl, *Theologia Moralis,* II, n. 462, p. 333.

precautions, somehow come to know the penitent, he is bound to sacramental silence exactly like the confessor. The same rule holds good if the penitent has consulted him personally or permitted the confessor to give his name. On this point scarcely any doubt has existed among the canonists and theologians.[19]

CONSULTANTS

Bound by the obligation of the seal are theologians (or anyone else) whom a confessor consults about a confessional case. St. Alphonsus listed three opinions about this question.[20] But the common and only tenable opinion today maintains that the consultant is bound by the seal, unless, of course, the penitent has expressly released him from this obligation.[21] The penitent's permission allowing the confessor to seek another's advice can be interpreted as allowing more than one interview with the consultant if this is necessary for the confessor to reach his judgment. This rests on the lawful presumption that the penitent's permission remains operative until the confessor renders his decision in the confessional case.[22]

What has been written here concerning the obligation of the consultant envisions instances wherein it is the confessor who, after hearing a confession, finds it necessary to seek another's counsel before he renders a decision. If, on the other hand, the penitent himself consults a priest about some confessional matter, would the latter be found by the seal? If the penitent consults a priest about a confession to be made to this same priest, the seal could bind the priest. The consultation could be the beginning of confession, *confessio inchoata.* If, however, a priest's advice is sought about a confession to be made to some other confessor, the priest-consultant does not contract the obligation of the seal.[23]

---

[19] Kurtscheid, *A History of the Seal of Confession,* pp. 243-244.

[20] Cf. *Theologia Moralis,* Lib. VI, n. 648.

[21] "Doctor consultus a confessario de licentia poenitentis, ex fere communi omnium sententia, tenetur sigillo sacramentali."—Conte a Coronata, *Institutiones Iuris Canonici,* IV, n. 2143, p. 634.

[22] Cf. St. Alphonsus, *op. cit.,* Lib. VI, n. 648.

[23] While most modern authors say without qualification that the seal does not oblige the consultant in this second case, Iorio regards the opinion as

A further distinction or clarification seems necessary regarding the first case, that is, when a penitent consults a priest and then seeks sacramental absolution from the same priest. In other words, the priest-consultant becomes the priest-confessor. In all such cases wherein confession follows consultation, must the consultation be considered as the beginning of the confession and, therefore, protected by the seal? Undoubtedly such consultation *can* constitute the *confessio inchoata* and thereby engender the obligation of the seal. But it does not seem correct to maintain that all such consultation necessarily constitutes such a *confessio inchoata.* That result depends upon the intention of the one seeking counsel. The same advice could conceivably be sought in the confidence of the internal non-sacramental forum by a penitent whose intention here and now of receiving direction from the priest neither includes nor excludes but abstracts from any subsequent petition for sacramental absolution. Circumstances would sometimes clearly reveal the petitioner's intention. At other times the priest could learn which forum was involved only by making some remark to clarify the issue or by actually asking the person some question which would manifest his mind. In doubt, of course, the presumption must favor the seal. While many authors do not enunciate this distinction, it is noted in the following texts:

> Item [sigillo tenetur] theologus consultus a confessario, de licentia poenitentis; vel a poenitente de confessione eidem facienda et sic inchoata; non de facienda vel facta alteri. Nec si poenitens sacerdotem consulat, v. gr., de casu speciali, quin de confessione ipsi facienda cogitet; et post acceptum consilium eidem confiteatur.[24]

> Ille tamen quem ipse paenitens consulit circa confessionem faciendam *solo secreto naturali* tenetur, nisi, propter manifestatam voluntatem, subinde eidem con-

at least more probable.—*Theologia Moralis* (Editio tertia recognita et emendata, 3 vols., Neapoli: M. D'Auria, 1946-1947), III, n. 621, p. 360. Some older authors held the opposite opinion on the grounds that otherwise confession would be rendered odious if the consultant disclosed any confidential information. St. Alphonsus replied that not confession but consultation would become odious.—Cf. *op. cit.,* Lib. VI, n. 649.

[24] Regatillo, *Ius Sacramentarium,* n. 551, pp. 319-320.

fitendi, consultatio rationem *inchoatae* confessionis induere videatur.[25]

But, one may ask, what if a man were to go to a priest who is vesting for Mass, and, in order to put an end to his worrying, explain certain severe temptations which he has just experienced? Is this to be deemed sacramental confession? It is sacramental on one condition: namely, that the man desires the priest to give him absolution, in case he judges it necessary or advisable. If, on the other hand, a person confesses his sins by letter to a priest in another town, there would be no sacramental secrecy involved. Why is this? The confession, in order to be sacramental, must be made to a priest who is actually present.[26]

THOSE WHO OVERHEAR A CONFESSION

One who overhears another's confession, whether culpably or inculpably, is bound by the seal. If, however, the penitent realizes he is speaking so loudly as to be overheard and yet continues to do so, he thereby relinquishes his claim to sacramental secrecy.[27] If a bystander intentionally listens to another's confession, he not only is bound by the seal but has already violated it. If several bystanders overhear the same confession, they would violate the seal even by speaking about the confessional matter among themselves.

St. Alphonsus and others maintained that in cases of necessity, such as might occur during a shipwreck, at a fire, in a battle, etc., when the penitent cannot confess his sins without being overheard by others, all who hear such a confession are bound by the seal.[28] Ballerini-Palmieri disagree. They argue that in these circumstances no one is bound to express any particular sin, but can

---

[25] Vermeersch, *Theologia Moralis,* III, n. 463, p. 297.

[26] Healy, "The Seal of Confession," *Review for Religious,* II (1943), 179.

[27] "If, however, a penitent in the hearing of others, confesses in a loud voice and knows that others can hear him, he has forfeited of his own will the right to sacramental secrecy, but not necessarily to all secrecy, for the natural secret may still have to be preserved."—Davis, *Moral and Pastoral Theology,* III, 320.

[28] "Et sic pariter tenentur ad sigillum adstantes, in quorum praesentia confessio fit ex necessitate, puta in naufragio, conflictu, etc."—*Op. cit.,* Lib. VI, n. 647. Cf. also Suarez, *De Poenitentia,* disp. 33, sect. 4, n. 7; De Lugo, *De Sacramento Poenitentiae,* disp. 23, sect. 2, n. 39.

instead simply make a generic confession of sin.[29] But neither is anyone bound to use an interpreter in order to express his sins in a specific way; and yet, an interpreter used for this purpose during confession is obliged by sacramental secrecy.

THOSE WHO WRITE ANOTHER'S CONFESSION

Penitents who cannot express their sins orally are not obliged to employ the extraordinary means of writing out their sins in order to effect a materially integral confession. However, under certain circumstances, a penitent may choose to do so.[30] If such a person were unable to write for himself but engaged another to do so, would the scribe be bound by the seal? Some authors state without qualification that a person who writes out another's confession is obliged by the seal.[31] Others are more restrictive, stating that the scribe is bound by the seal if he writes the sins during confession, but not if he writes them before confession.[32]

THOSE TO WHOM MATTER PROTECTED BY THE SEAL IS REVEALED

Those to whom a confessor (or anyone else bound by the seal) directly or indirectly, advertently or inadvertently, culpably or inculpably, reveals matter protected by the seal are likewise bound to sacramental secrecy.[33] For example, if A, having overheard

[29] *Opus Theologicum Morale,* V, n. 965.

[30] Cf. Cappello, *Tractatus Canonico-Moralis de Sacramentis,* II, n. 136, pp. 123-124.

[31] "Hinc ad sigillum tenentur . . . qui scribunt confessionem rudium, vel ignorantium linguam confessarii, praesertim si alio modo confessio peragi non possit."—Iorio, *op. cit.,* III, n. 617, p. 358.

[32] "One who acts as scribe in writing out before confession the list of sins or one sin for another is not bound by the seal, but if he acted as scribe during a confession he would be bound by the seal."—Davis, *op. cit.,* III, 320.

"Non nulli obligationem extendunt ad eum qui ante confessionem peccata rudis scripserit, quod potius negandum esse arbitramur, quia operam, ceterum non praeceptam, extra confessionem praestat, nec apud ipsum confessio inchoata censeri potest."—Vermeersch, *Theologia Moralis,* III, n. 463, p. 297.

[33] "Ratio est quia *res transit ad alios cum onere suo* . . . et proinde scientia confessionis, velut depositum sigillo munitum, omnes, ad quos pervenit, ad sigillum constringit."—P. Rota, *Enchiridion Confessarii et Judicis Ecclesiastici,* pars. 1, sect. 1, cap. 2, n. 12.

B's confession without realizing his obligation to secrecy, then conveys knowledge of B's confession to C, C is thereby bound by the seal of confession. If C should none the less reveal the matter to D, D would also be bound, and so forth *usque ad infinitum.* The same would hold true if a priest in consequence of his lack of caution were to perpetrate an indirect violation of the seal, for example, while preaching. All of his hearers would be bound by the seal, so that they could not even speak of the matter among themselves.[34]

ONE WHO READS WRITTEN MATTER PROTECTED BY THE SEAL

Because of an intimate connection with confession, certain written matter enjoys the protection of the seal. If anyone were to read written matter of this nature, he would be bound to sacramental secrecy concerning the contents.

It is beyond all question that written matter protected by the seal includes letters sent to the Sacred Penitentiary, to the local ordinary, or to some other superior concerning reserved cases. Such letters may be petitions for the faculty of absolving from some reserved sin or censure, or else they are sent to satisfy the subsequent recourse demanded by canons 2252 and 2254. If so, these documents enjoy the protection of the seal whether they are sent by the confessor or by the penitent.

> Nihil refert utrum litterae a confessario, an a poenitente mittantur. At omnino requiritur, ad obligationem sigilli sacramentalis inducendum, ut litterae mittantur revera a confessario vel a poenitente *qua tali* idque manifesto constet.[35]

Similarly falling under the seal are the replies made to such letters by the Sacred Penitentiary, by the local ordinary, or by other superiors, whatever the case may be.[36]

A second type of written material which could conceivably fall

---

[34] Cf. Conte a Coronata, *Institutiones Iuris Canonici,* IV, n. 2143, p. 633; Cappello, *op. cit.,* II, n. 596, p. 616.

[35] Cappello, *Tractatus Canonico-Moralis de Sacramentis,* II, n. 596, p. 618.

[36] Cf. Iorio, *Theologia Moralis,* III, n. 620, pp. 359-360.

under the secrecy of the seal is a confession made in writing. In certain circumstances a penitent may confess in writing rather than orally. (In either case, the confession must be *inter praesentes.*) At other times a penitent could indeed confess orally, but with the aid of a written list of sins.[37] If some other party were to read such a written confession or list of sins, would he be bound by the seal? Authors answer as follows:

(a) If the list of sins is merely an aid to facilitate one's examination of conscience and is not meant to be used during the actual confession, it does not merit the protection of the seal. One who reads such a list is no more bound by the seal than one who hears a penitent's audible examination of conscience.[38]

(b) If a list of sins has been prepared for its later use during confession but is read by a third party prior to the actual confession, authors disagree as to its coverage by the seal. Some claim that if the written confession has been prepared, for example, by a mute person, then, inasmuch as it is a means which he is free to employ in order to make a materially integral confession, it merits the protection of the seal.[39] Others disagree on the grounds that even the mute person is not obliged to write out his sins before confession.[40]

(c) Some authors mention that a written confession given to

---

[37] Whether or not this is advisable is not at issue here.

[38] Cf. De Lugo, *De Sacramento Poenitentiae,* disp. 23, sect. 2, n. 47.

[39] E.g., Lehmkuhl: "Si poenitenti scriptio necessarium medium est confessionem integram faciendi, ante ipsam confessionem chartam legere, est sacramentalem notitiam invadere, atque ita sigillo obstringi."—*Theologia Moralis,* II, n. 464, p. 334.

[40] E.g., Vermeersch: *"Nec si ante usum pro confessione legatur,* contra sigillum peccabitur. Nequit enim privilegiatum sigillum confessionis sacramentalis extendi ad media non necessaria quae confessionem praecedunt. Aliter dicendum foret si in ipsa confessione rudis peccata sua alicui dictaret. Cfr. Lehmkuhl . . . qui tamen sigillo protectam dicit chartam in qua paenitens peccata sua scripsit, si scriptio necessarium fuerit paenitenti medium confessionem integram faciendi. Verum paenitens numquam cogitur scriptionem ante confessionem conficere."—*Theologia Moralis,* III, n. 463, pp. 297-298.

the confessor before the confession but with a view to subsequent confession falls under the seal.[41]

(d) One who reads the written confession of another during the confession itself is bound by the seal. Authors agree on this.

(e) One who reads a written confession left in the confessional is bound by the seal. Some authors make this statement without further qualification.[42] Others hold this to be true if the written confession is left in the confessional by the confessor.[43] Davis contended that if it is left in the confessional by the penitent, it is probably not matter of the sacramental seal.[44] Cappello points out that, if it is uncertain whether the penitent or the confessor left the written account in the confessional, a person would endanger the seal by reading it.[45]

(f) If the written confession is lost by the confessor, one who reads it is bound by the seal.[46]

(g) If the written confession was actually used by the penitent during confession, but was then retained, discarded, or lost by him after confession, it is outside the secrecy of the seal. Ferreres (1861-1936) qualified this statement by stating that the written

---

[41] E.g., Davis: "If it [i.e., the written confession] was given to a confessor as such before confession with a view to future confession it comes within the scope of sacramental matter."—*Moral and Pastoral Theology,* III, 321.

Iorio: "Eadem de causa sigillo tenetur qui legit chartam confessario iam traditam intuitu confessionis apud ipsum peragendae, etsi de facto haec nondum fuerit instituta."—*Theologia Moralis,* III, n. 620, p. 360.

[42] "Card. De Lugo . . . non limitat, *si charta amissa sit ab ipso Confessario,* sed (*De Poenit.* Disp. 23, n. 48.) generatim dicit: *Imo licet post absolutionem aliquis invenisset eam in confessionali, probabile videtur, quod teneretur ad sigillum: quia illa videtur esse ipsa confessio manens.*"—Gury, *Compendium Theologiae Moralis,* II, n. 653, p. 632, footnote (a).

[43] E.g., Wouters: "Tenetur sigillo sacramentali . . . probabiliter, qui legit chartam post confessionem a confessario relictam; quia in casu videtur dici posse [legentem], mediante confessario, accepisse notitiam confessionis." —*Manuale Theologiae Moralis,* II, n. 436, p. 343.

[44] Cf. *op. cit.,* III, 321.

[45] Cf. *Tractatus Canonico-Moralis de Sacramentis,* II, n. 596, p. 617.

[46] "One who reads the written confession of another . . . if the written confession . . . has been mislaid or lost by the confessor, is bound by the seal."—Davis, *op. cit.,* III, 321.

confession would be protected by the seal if it had been lost by the penitent before he was able, within the realm of the morally feasible, to destroy it.[47] Chrétien writes in a similar fashion that the written confession is no longer protected by the seal if it is lost by the penitent through his own carelessness.[48]

PENITENT

Since the seal is intended to protect the penitent and not the confessor, the penitent is not bound to sacramental secrecy concerning his own confession. But the penitent would violate natural secrecy if, by needlessly revealing such things as the penance imposed or the advice given by the confessor, he were to lower the esteem in which the confessor is held by others, or to subject him to ridicule. Others would not know the reasons why a certain penance or advice was given, and the confessor would be helpless in the defense of himself.[49]

> A penitent is not bound by the sacramental seal in respect of his own confession, but he may be bound by an obligation to keep a natural secret, if the confessor's action or advice falls into that category, and his obligation is greater than that of others. He will sin grievously if, without reason, he seriously diminish the esteem of his confessor. At the same time, every confessor will use the greatest prudence in his treatment of penitents, never saying what he would not wish to be repeated.[50]

---

[47] Cf. *Compendium Theologiae Moralis,* II, n. 707, p. 451.
[48] Cf. *De Sigillo Sacramentali,* p. 105.
[49] Cf. Ballerini-Palmieri, *Opus Theologicum Morale,* V, n. 975, pp. 527-528.
[50] Davis, *op. cit.,* III, 321.

CHAPTER V

The Inviolability of the Seal

The sacramental seal, both as derived from the divine law and as defined in canon 889, is inviolable. It demands observance always, in every case, with no exceptions. Even the Roman Pontiff is powerless to dispense from it. No cause, however great, excuses from its observance. Its obligation does not expire with the passing of time, but continues on even after the death of the penitent. It demands silence from the confessor in respect to everyone, including the penitent himself outside confession.

TWO MITIGATIONS OF THE SEAL'S ABSOLUTENESS

Two mitigations of the seal's absoluteness must, however, be mentioned. First, while the confessor cannot speak of confessional matters to the penitent outside of confession without the latter's permission, he is free to do so in subsequent confessions. It is not contrary to the law of the seal for the confessor to mention in subsequent confessions what the penitent has disclosed in previous ones. Similarly, the confessor can speak to the penitent of confessional matters after absolution has been imparted but before the penitent departs from the confessional, inasmuch as a moral unity with the confession still exists.[1]

Secondly, the seal's absolute inviolability does not mean that the penitent cannot release the confessor from the obligation. With the permission of the penitent, the confessor can speak of confessional matters to others. Canon 1757, § 3, 2°, presupposes this fact. Suarez, De Lugo, and others point out, however, that this

---

[1] "Communiter tamen dicunt doctores, licitum esse confessario loqui de auditis in confessione cum poenitente statim post absolutionem antequam ille discedat; quia, licet sacramentum sit completum, tamen judicium adhuc moraliter perseverat."—St. Alphonsus, *Theologia Moralis,* Lib. VI, n. 652.

statement has a twofold meaning.[2] To say that the penitent grants the confessor permission to disclose confessional matter can mean two things:

(a) FIRST MEANING: What the penitent tells the priest in confession, he can also tell him outside of confession. The same content would then be the object of not only the priest's sacramental knowledge but also his extra-sacramental knowledge. The priest would not and could not be bound by the seal in respect to his extra-sacramental awareness of this information. Furthermore, those to whom the priest communicates this extra-sacramental information, would not and could not be bound by the seal regarding it.

While it is beyond dispute that the penitent can furnish the priest with extra-sacramental knowledge of what he has already confessed, there is some question concerning the manner in which this can be done. The difficulty lies in whether the penitent who has already disclosed certain information in confession can effect the extra-sacramental disclosure of it by the mere expression of his consent, or whether he must once again repeat the entire information outside of confession. Suarez, De Lugo, and others maintained that the entire repetition of what was said in confession was not required before the confessor could obtain extra-sacramental knowledge of it. The penitent could simply state that what he had told the priest in confession he wished the priest to know also in an extra-sacramental way. They based their argument on the fact that the reverse process was allowed. If the penitent has manifested his sins to the priest outside of confession, he could subsequently confess them simply by stating that he accused himself of all the sins previously disclosed to the priest. There was no need for a full repetition of them. The same should

[2] "Circa secundum punctum de locutione cum facultate poenitentis, duo sunt distinguenda, quae ab auctoribus confunduntur. Aliud enim est, quod poenitens res semel dictas in confessione, iterum extra confessionem dicat. Aliud vero, quod servato eodem sigillo, et eadem scientia, det facultatem loquendi ex illa."—Suarez, *De Poenitentia,* disp. 23, sect. 5, n. 4; cf. also De Lugo, *De Sacramento Poenitentiae,* disp. 23, sect. 5, n. 133.

hold true when the process is reversed.[3] De Lugo mentioned Vasquez (1549-1604) as holding the contrary opinion.[4] Cappello also demands a full recounting of the sins outside of confession in order to effect the extra-sacramental awareness of them:

> Nec sane in potestate poenitentis est, quod res cognita in *foro Dei,* fiat cognita in *foro humano,* sine nova atque expressa eiusdem rei communicatione in ipso foro humano facta.
>
> Nec satis est per se, quod poenitens, in actu confessionis aut extra, dicat sacerdoti: *omnia quae in confessione tibi dico vel dixi, extra confessionem dicta habeantur.*
>
> Poenitens seu fidelis extra confessionem omnia singillatim repetat, quae opportune vel necessario in foro *humano* cum aliis communicanda videntur. Haec norma practice *semper* servetur.[5]

Many, if not most, of the modern authors, however, accept the opinion held by Suarez and De Lugo.[6] The writer believes that canon 1757, § 3, 2°, seems to presuppose that the penitent is able to release the confessor from the secrecy of the seal without repeating all of the confession extra-sacramentally.

(b) SECOND MEANING: What the penitent manifests to the confessor in confession he can allow the confessor to disclose or use outside of confession, in the sense, however, that the knowledge remains sacramental rather than that it becomes extra-sacra-

---

[3] "Dicit Durandus necessarium esse ut omnia singillatim repetat, nulla facta mentione confessionis. Sed non existimo esse necessarium; unico enim verbo dicere potest: Omnia, quae in confessione dixi, extra confessionem sint dicta; quia illud unum verbum hic et nunc sufficienter significat omnia, sicut in superioribus e contrario dicebamus, posse aliquem uno verbo plura confiteri simili modo."—Suarez, *loc. cit.;* cf. also, De Lugo, *ibid.,* n. 137.

[4] *Ibid.,* n. 136.

[5] *Tractatus Canonico-Moralis de Sacramentis,* II, n. 621. 1° 11°, pp. 642-644. Cf. also, Genicot-Salsmans, *Institutiones Theologiae Moralis,* II, n. 388, p. 269.

[6] E.g., Davis: "The very general permission given by a penitent of treating everything said in confession as said out of confession is equivalent to extra-sacramental communication of knowledge."—*Moral and Pastoral Theology,* III, 327-328; Vermeersch: "Vel sigillum a paenitente aufertur sive *formaliter* dicendo: 'omnia sint quasi dicta extra confessionem,' sive *virtualiter,* ut cum ipse paenitens, repetendo quae in confessione dixit, suppeditet notitiam extrasacramentalem."—*Theologia Moralis,* III, n. 469, p. 301.

mental. While the penitent allows the confessor to make extra-sacramental reference to confessional information, nevertheless the information itself still remains the object of the seal; it does not become extra-sacramental.[7] Consequently, all those to whom the information is communicated are bound by the seal regarding it. Furthermore, the penitent's permission is revocable in this case, whereas if the knowledge becomes extra-sacramental, as explained under (a), the penitent is unable to restore it under the seal by revoking his permission. Not all authors have agreed that the penitent is able to do what has been explained thus far under (b). That the penitent can do so was called the common opinion by Suarez and De Lugo. They mentioned Scotus and others as holding the opposite opinion.[8] Doronzo writes that the affirmative opinion, the one upholding the penitent's ability to allow the confessor to disclose confessional knowledge *as such,* was more commonly held by the older authors and is most generally held by the modern authors.[9]

Among present day authors, however, Cappello dissents. Cappello argues that the penitent *as such* cannot grant permission to the confessor *as such* to speak of confessional information outside of that tribunal. He can, of course, permit the confessor to approach a superior for necessary faculties or to consult a theologian about a confessional case, but these actions are still a part of confession, *confessio continuata.* But the penitent has not the power to permit the confessor's speaking of confessional matters to others outside of confession in such a way that the information would remain the object of sacramental knowledge and the recipients of it would be bound by the seal.[10]

---

[7] ". . . ita dari potest [licentia] ut paenitens ius ad sigillum servet vel amittat."—Vermeersch, *loc. cit.*

[8] Cf. Suarez, *op. cit.,* disp. 33, sect. 5, nn. 5-6; De Lugo, *op. cit.,* disp. 23, sect. 5, nn. 132-133.

[9] "Affirmant vero communius antiquiores et communissime moderni"—*De Poenitentia,* II, 844

[10] "Poenitens *qua talis* nequit confessario *qua confessario* concedere licentiam loquendi de auditis in confessione. Nam confessarius quidquid cognoscit in confessione, cognoscit *ut Deus,* ac proinde *in foro Dei,* iuxta S. Thomam.

"Cum autem poenitens dat licentiam loquendi confessario, hic notitiam

It seems to the writer that Cappello's reasoning forces an untenable conclusion. If a confessor were to violate the seal, he would be revealing *in foro humano* what he learned *in foro Dei.* And yet no one would claim that the seal would not oblige his listeners for the reason that the revelation was made *in foro humano.* If the seal obliges the recipient of confessional information in the case wherein a confessor without authorization speaks of confessional knowledge *in foro humano,* it seems consistent to maintain that the seal can continue to be of obligation when the confessor speaks *in foro humano* with the penitent's permission.

In summary, the penitent can allow the confessor to reveal sacramental information in the two ways explained above under (a) and (b). This is admitted by most of the modern authors. If done in the first manner, that of (a), the permission then amounts to an extra-sacramental communication of the knowledge; such permission is irrevocable, and the recipients of the information are not bound by the seal. If the permission, on the other hand, is of the second type, namely, that described in (b), the information remains under the seal, and all those to whom it is communicated must be advised of their obligation to sacramental secrecy concerning it. Consequently, authors point out the expediency of receiving more than the permission described in (b) in cases wherein the confessor undertakes any commission, such as making restitution for the penitent.[11]

---

rerum percipit *ut homo,* secundum ipsum *Angelicum,* ideoque *in foro humano.* Porro toto coelo differt profecto, quod sacerdos rem aliquam cognoscat *qua Deus* vel *qua homo,* quod fidelis loquatur in *foro Dei* vel in *foro humano.*

"Eo ipso quod poenitens facultatem loquendi de accusatis in confessione concederet confessario, hic *qua homo* sciret, ut supra dictum est, et *qua homo* loqueretur cum aliis, qui proinde lege sigilli sacramentalis nec tenerentur nec teneri possent. Quam rerum conditionem nullo pacto sua voluntate sive intentione mutare poenitens valeret.

"Unde minus recte quidam DD. dicunt, licentiam loquendi a poenitente ita confessario concedi posse, ut is, quocum res communicatur, ad sigillum teneatur."—*Op. cit.,* II, n. 621, pp. 641-642.

[11] "Quapropter si confessarius loco poenitentis debitorum remissionem petiit ac propterea cum illius facultate peccatum furti etc. domino laeso aperuit, ipse dominus huius furti notitiam *sub sigillo sacramentali* habet: quia apud poenitentem est, concedere facultatem notitiae in sacramento a

TYPE OF PERMISSION REQUIRED

Several qualities are demanded in the penitent's permission which allows the confessor to speak of what has been confessed. The permission must be:

(a) EXPRESSED—The penitent must expressly grant his consent. In so delicate and important a matter, presumed permissions are ruled out. The confessor "is obliged to assume for certain the penitent's unwillingness that confessional matter should be revealed . . . without express permission."[12] Even if the revelation by the confessor would seem to work to the penitent's advantage, the confessor cannot presume the necessary permission. Otherwise penitents would fear that the confessor might presume permission unwarrantably.[13] If, however, in conversation with his confessor outside of confession the penitent speaks of his past confessions, he is thereby sufficiently expressing his consent for the confessor to speak to him about the confessional matter under discussion. But the permission extends only to the particular matter which the penitent brings up for discussion.[14]

(b) NOT REVOKED—If the penitent's permission actually amounts to an extra-sacramental communication of what he told in confession, as explained above, then no revocation of the permission is possible in the sense that the seal would again become operative. But if the penitent consents with the understanding that

---

confessario acceptae divulgandae aut *sub eodem sigillo* clausae, i.e. eo modo, quo confessarius eam tenet, aut laxiore modo. Sed quando cum restitutione, per confessarium facienda vel componenda, declaratio poenitentis necessaria est, vix videtur convenire, hoc negotium a confessario ita suscipi, ut tota illa notitia sub sigillo clausa maneat. Quare nisi poenitens licentiam det illius negotii liberius tractandi sub solo secreto naturali, confessarii est prospicere, num expediat cum tanto onere causam poenitentis apud alterum tractare."—Lehmkuhl, *Theologia Moralis,* II, n. 463, p. 333. Cf. also Vermeersch, *Theologia Moralis,* III, n. 463, p. 297.

[12] Davis, *Moral and Pastoral Theology,* III, 316.

[13] "Debet autem haec licentia esse non praesumpta, vel interpretativa; sed formalis et expressa. Alioquin saepius fingerent sibi talem licentiam confessarii contra veram poenitentis voluntatem."—De Lugo, *De Sacramento Poenitentiae,* disp. 23, sect. 5, n. 131.

[14] Cf. *loc. cit.*

the information remains sacramental, then he can at any time once again demand sacramental secrecy by revoking his grant.[15]

(c) SPONTANEOUS—The penitent must give his consent freely. If, for inducing the penitent to yield his consent, undue pressure or even reverential fear were allowed to be exerted, then the sacrament would to some extent become odious, which very thing the seal is expected to prevent.[16] This must not however be interpreted as a prohibition against the confessor's demanding an extra-sacramental manifestation of some matter by the penitent, even under the threat of denying absolution, if the case calls for such action.[17]

COROLLARIES

It will be useful to note several corollaries which pertain to the inviolability of the seal and to the permission of the penitent who wishes to relax the obligation:

(a) RESERVED CASES: Does the confessor need the penitent's permission in order to apply for faculties in reserved cases? If there is no danger whatsoever that the superior from whom the faculties are sought will come to know the identity of the penitent involved in the reserved case, then the confessor does not need the penitent's permission to seek such faculties.[18] In cases of re-

[15] Cf. St. Alphonsus, *Theologia Moralis,* Lib. VI, n. 651.

[16] Cf. *loc. cit.* In this regard, the II Plenary Council of Baltimore (1866) wrote as follows: "Nunquam a poenitente petat, multo minus importunis precibus extorqueat veniam, quae in Confessione audiit aliis revelandi, nec cum ipso quidem de iis extra tribunal loquendi. Si forte, vi legis divinae, vera et proprie dicta obligatio aliquid in Confessione dictum revelandi exorta fuerit, id per ipsum poenitentem fiat, vel per alium quem ipse elegerit. Nullo modo sacerdos id oneris ultro suscipiat, neque nisi invitus poenitenti id ab eo postulanti morem gerat."—*Concilii Plenarii Baltimorensis II Acta et Decreta,* decr. 290.

[17] "Sigillo non obstat, quominus confessarius communicationem vel denuntiationem extrasacramentaliter revera sub gravi faciendam urgeat, etiam sub denegata absolutione. Sed expedit, ut confessarius in tali casu eandem rem sibi iterum manifestari faciat extra confessionem, non vero petat, ut scientia, sacramentaliter iam accepta, extrasacramentaliter uti possit."—Hürth-Abellan, *De Sacramentis,* n. 429, p. 239.

[18] Cf. Cappello, *Tractatus Canonico-Moralis de Sacramentis,* II, n. 596, p. 615.

served sins, as distinguished from reserved censures, the reservation ceases if there is danger that the petition for faculties might result in a revelation of the penitent's identity.[19] Under such circumstances there would be no need for seeking additional faculties. Without the penitent's permission, however, the confessor could not petition faculties to absolve from *reserved censures* if there is any danger of disclosing the penitent's identity to the superior.

The Sacred Penitentiary issued the following warning concerning the handling of occult cases:

> Although natural prudence itself demands that occult cases which pertain to the forum of conscience be proposed directly to the Sacred Penitentiary or to His Eminence, the Cardinal Major Penitentiary, in sealed letters and without giving the names of the parties concerned, yet there are some confessors who have the hardihood to present such cases by open letters to be handed to procurators or so-called agents.
>
> In order to put an end entirely to a practice so gravely unbecoming, the Sacred Penitentiary wishes expressly to warn all persons concerned never again to dare do anything of this kind, but to send such letters and all others which may later need to be added to them for the purpose of giving opportune notices or supplementary information, directly to the Sacred Penitentiary itself or to His Eminence, the Cardinal Major Penitentiary, either through the public mail, or, if they wish to make use of the service of an agent, through the agent in a special envelope securely sealed.[20]

(b) NECESSARY CONSULTATION: Is the penitent's permission required before a confessor can seek another's consultation regarding a confessional case? The same distinction as in reserved cases must be applied to consultation. If the confessor can consult another priest in such a way that there is no danger of revealing

---

[19] Cf. c. 900, 2°.

[20] Bouscaren, *The Canon Law Digest* (4 vols., Milwaukee: Bruce Publishing Co., Vol. I, 1934; Vol. II, 1943; Vol. III, 1954; Vol. IV [Bouscaren-O'Connor], 1958), II, 219. The admonition appeared in the *Acta Apostolicae Sedis,* XXVII (1953), 62.

the identity of the penitent, then the penitent's permission is not necessary. Otherwise it must be obtained before any consultation is allowable. If possible, the confessor should consult a priest to whom the penitent is unknown. If this is impossible and there is danger to the seal, the confessor cannot proceed without the penitent's consent. Sometimes, however, the confessor will be able to preclude all danger of revelation by proposing a fictitious case to the consultant or by interjecting fictitious circumstances and details in so far as this is feasible. In any case, if there remains any danger to the seal, the confessor cannot consult another without the penitent's permission. One author suggests the following rules concerning consultation: "Don't consult unless it is necessary. . . . Don't ask penitents for permission to consult unless this is really necessary. . . . When you do consult without permission be sure there is no danger that the consultant will identify the penitent. . . . Even when you have permission to consult, reveal no more than is necessary."[21]

(c) REPAIRING CONFESSIONAL DEFECTS: At times a priest may be confronted with the problem of correcting some defect or mistake made by him during the hearing of confessions. These defects, for example, may concern the validity of absolution, the question of restitution, and the like. What is the relation between the obligation of the seal and the duty of correcting confessional defects?

A basic principle is that the necessity of repairing defects never justifies a violation of the seal.[22] It would not violate the seal, however, for the confessor in a subsequent confession to speak to the penitent of the defect even without the latter's permission. The problem of the seal arises when the correcting of the defect necessitates the priest's speaking of it to the penitent outside of confession. Must he obtain the penitent's permission before doing so? He must obtain it whenever matter protected by the seal is included in the extra-sacramental conversation. For example, if a

---

[21] Kelly, *The Good Confessor*, pp. 49-51. Cf. also, Cappello, *op. cit.*, II, n. 624, pp. 647-648.

[22] "Nulla violatio sigilli sacramentalis necessitate reparandi defectum excusatur."—Vermeersch, *Theologia Moralis*, III, n. 508, p. 329.

confessor mistakenly advises a penitent who confesses a theft that he is not obliged to make restitution, the confessor could not speak of this mistake to the penitent outside of confession unless he first obtained the latter's permission to do so. This is so because matter protected by the seal, namely the theft, would necessarily be referred to in the extra-sacramental conversation. On the other hand, if the extra-sacramental conversation does not involve matter protected by the seal, then the penitent's permission is not required. For example, if the confessional defect consists in the fact that the confessor recited an invalid form of absolution, the confessor would not need the penitent's permission to notify him outside of confession of the invalid absolution. The fact that the confessor erred in pronouncing the words of absolution does not, at least in itself, fall under the seal. Consequently, he needs no express permission to speak of this defect to the penitent outside of confession.[23]

SOME THINGS THE CONFESSOR MUST DO OR SAY TO PROTECT THE SEAL

(a) A confessor who is questioned about matter protected by the seal must deny, even under oath, that he has heard of or knows anything about the matter in question. His justification for such an assertion is that he actually has no human or communicable knowledge about the information being sought.[24] If such a reply,

[23] "Alii defectus corrigi nequeunt, nisi confessarius cum poenitente loquatur, v.g. si indebite ad restitutionem eum obligavit vel ab ea facienda deobligavit. Tunc videndum imprimis, num sit loquendum de re, quae est sub sigillo sacramentali necne. Si primum, loqui non licet, nisi prius petita et obtenta fuerit licentia poenitentis; si alterum, id non requiritur, saltem per se et generatim loquendo.

". . . generatim quando nullitatis ratio fuit defectus ab ipso confessario admissus, necesse non est ut praevie exquiratur a poenitente licentia loquendi; cum ad *sigilli* materiam nullatenus pertineat, quod confessarius dicat se non absolvisse aut in danda absolutione errasse.

"At si ratio nullitatis fuit defectus poenitentis, eius *licentia* petenda est, quia potest esse invitus quominus huiusmodi defectus ei in memoriam revocetur."—Cappello, *op. cit.*, II, nn. 533-534, pp. 540-541.

[24] "Confessarius interroganti de auditis in confessione respondere debet se nihil scire; idque etiam respondere debet etsi interrogatur et provocatur ad respondendum ut minister Dei et sine aequivocatione et restrictione mentali,

however, would lead others to suspect that the information actually had been confessed or that the penitent failed to make an integral confession, then the confessor should answer in a different manner. Perhaps the best manner of handling such questions is to reprove the inquirer for raising the question, unless this too would cause suspicions about the actual confession.[25]

(b) A priest need not confess some sin of his own if by doing so he would endanger the seal. The obligation of the seal takes precedence over the obligation of making a materially integral confession.[26]

(c) A hospital chaplain who is asked whether a particular penitent wishes to receive Holy Communion should direct the inquirer to the penitent himself for an answer. If a priest does this in all cases, he will avoid complications concerning the seal which could arise in instances wherein he was unable to grant absolution.[27]

(d) If sick call registers include a record of whether or not the patient confessed, the confessor must indicate that a penitent made his confession even though absolution was denied. "In some hospitals and parishes it seems to be customary for the priest who has visited a sick person to check certain items on a chart. . . . I see no particular good to be derived from marking on such a chart that the penitent went to confession. And in some cases it might be misleading, because, if confession is checked, it must be checked for all who went to confession, whether they received absolution or not."[28]

---

scilicet non necessaria, idque etiam iureiurando confirmare potest."—Conte a Coronata, *Institutiones Iuris Canonici,* IV, n. 2143, pp. 632-633.

[25] "*Practice* huiusmodi interrogationes declinandae sunt silentio vel increpatione interrogantis, hac similive formula adhibita: ad has interrogationes non est, quod respondeam. Sed cavendum est ne confessarius id agat in iis adiunctis, in quibus declinando clarum responsum, celandae veritatis suspicionem ingereret."—Cappello, *op. cit.,* II, n. 595, p. 613.

[26] "Confessarius, qui suum peccatum confiteri non potest sine laesione sigilli, illud omittere *debet.* Longe gravior enim est obligatio sigilli, quam obligatio integre confitendi, a qua causae multae excusant. Sed verum periculum laedendi sigillum raro aderit, dummodo in confessione non dicatur, nisi quod necessarium est ad speciem peccati declarandi."—Cappello, *op. cit.,* II, n. 595, p. 614.

[27] Cf. *loc. cit.*

[28] Kelly, *op. cit.,* p. 48.

CHAPTER VI

VIOLATIONS OF CANON 889 AND THE CORRESPONDING PENALTIES ENACTED IN CANON 2369

Canons 889 and 2369 of the Code are parallel passages. Canon 889 enunciates an obligation and canon 2369 enacts penalties for those who violate this same obligation. It is the seal as defined in canon 889 that is fortified with the protective penal sanctions of canon 2369. This is evident from the following considerations:

(a) The Code defines the seal only in terms of the *non-proditio peccatoris* as stated in canon 889. Some authors conclude that this is the only sense in which the expression "sacramental seal" can be used in its proper meaning; others admit this to be the seal in its strict sense, but give it also a broader or second proper meaning, which embraces the obligation delineated not only in canon 889 but also in canon 890. The seal as defined in canon 889 is either the only possible proper definition of the term, or at least the strict meaning of the term. If it is the only meaning, then it is beyond question that canon 2369 has this meaning in mind. If it is the stricter meaning, although not the exclusive one, then canon 2369 must still be regarded as having this meaning in mind. In penal matters—and canon 2369 concerns penalties—the term must be interpreted strictly. In either case, therefore, the seal to which canon 2369 adverts is coextensive with the seal as defined in canon 889—the *non-proditio peccatoris*.

(b) In the second paragraph of canon 2369, explicit reference is made to the second paragraph of canon 889. Those who violate the law of canon 889, § 2, are liable to the penalties enacted in canon 2369, § 2. This certainly gives at least some additional indication that canon 2369, § 1, has in mind the seal to which canon 889, § 1, adverts. Since there is this foundation for limiting the seal as delineated in the penal canon to the seal as defined in canon 889, it is contrary to canon 19 to extend the acceptance of the term in penal matters beyond canon 889, for example, by making violators of canon 890 subject to the penalties established for indirect violations of the seal. Some authors do this.[1]

(c) The ordinary pre-Code penalty was applicable only to those who betrayed the sinner by revealing his sin (*proditio peccatoris*), and not to those who made other improper use of confessional knowledge. *At best,* it remains doubtful whether the Code extends the nature of the delict so that it embraces the forbidden use of confessional knowledge. On such a basis, the extension must be rejected in virtue of canon 6, 4°.

(d) In Gasparri's *Schema Codicis,* the original draft of canon 2369, § 1, of the *Code* reads as follows:

> Censura specialissimo modo reservata tenet etiam confessarios qui praescriptum can. 162, *De Rebus,* directe violare praesumpserint; qui vero indirecte [etc.]—can. 176, *De Delictis et Poenis.*

In the *Schema Codicis,* can. 162, *De Rebus,* is the text of canon 889, § 1, of the *Code.*[2] This offers a further corroboration that the penalties for violations of the seal are established simply and exclusively for violations of the law enacted in canon 889.

In this dissertation, the seal as defined in canon 889 has been called the canonical seal. It is for violations of the canonical seal that one is liable to the canonical penalties enacted in canon 2369. This is true regardless of whether or not the term "seal" can also be properly employed in a broader sense in theological usage. It remains, therefore, to examine the ways in which the law of

---

[1] E.g.: "Violatio *indirecta,* quae etiam in imprudenti usu notitiae ex confessione acceptae contineri potest, est quoque delictum confessarii dumtaxat proprium."—Chelodi, *Ius Canonicum de Delictis et Poenis,* n. 462, p. 345.

An example of the contrary opinion is as follows: "Ut violatio indirecta sigilli non est habendus usus scientiae ex confessione acquisitae cum gravamine poenitentis, excluso quovis revelatione periculo. Qui usus a can. 890 prohibetur, at nullis poenis additis."—De Meester, *Juris Canonici et Juris Canonico-Civilis Compendium* (Nova editio ad normam C. I. C., 3 vols. in 4, Brugis: Sumpt. et typ. Societatis S. Augustini, 1921-1928), III-2, n. 1873, p. 274.

[2] Cf. *Schema Codicis Iuris Canonici* (4 vols. in 2, Romae: Typis Polyglottis Vaticanis, 1912-1914, IV, can. 176, *De Delictis et Poenis;* III, can. 162, *De Rebus.*

canon 889, that is the law regarding the canonical seal, can be violated, and then to outline the corresponding penalties enacted in canon 2369.

VIOLATIONS OF CANON 889

The seal as defined in canon 889 entails the duty of not betraying the sinner (*caveat ne prodat peccatorem*). This duty one would violate by revealing conjunctively the sinner and his sin.[3] It is necessary to note several points which clarify the notion of the phrase "to reveal conjunctively the sinner and his sin":

(a) "To reveal" in this sense means to disclose something *to a third party*. It consists in the communication of a secret to a person other than the person who entrusted the secret (the penitent).[4] While the confessor would sin by speaking of confessional matter to the penitent outside of confession, he would not be guilty of the technical *proditio peccatoris* of canon 889. In the terminology adopted in this dissertation, he would violate the divine seal, but not the canonical seal.

A number of pre-Code authors explicitly stated that the revelation which makes a confessor liable to the canonical penalties, that is, the revelation which constitutes a *proditio peccatoris*, demands disclosure to a third party.[5] Authors after the Code imply the same either by classifying unauthorized conversation with the penitent outside of confession about confessional matters as a forbidden use of confessional knowledge (canon 890), or by stating that such unlawful conversation on the confessor's part does not render him liable to the penalties enacted in canon 2369.[6] How-

---

[3] Cf. *supra*, p. 17.

[4] "Revelare proprie is dicitur, qui secretum sibi commissum alteri pandit; nam si cum eo, qui secretum commisit, de secreto loquitur, per se nihil ei revelat, et secretum non prodit."—P. Rota, *Enchiridion Confessarii et Judicis Ecclesiastici*, pars 1, sect. 1, cap. 6, n. 68.

[5] Cf. *supra*, p. 19.

[6] E.g., "Locutio cum paenitente *extra* confessionem, sine paenitentis licentia, est *prohibitus usus* scientiae sacramentalis."—Vermeersch, *Theologia Moralis*, III, n. 470, p. 302.

"Si confessarius, sine licentia poenitentis, cum ipso loqueretur extra tribunal Poenitentiae de auditis in confessione, peccaret quidem, at non in-ever, just as some authors consider violations of the law of canon 890 as meriting the penalties established for indirect violations of the seal, so also do they contend that the confessor's unlawful conversation with the penitent about confessional matters renders him liable to the penalties for indirect violations.[7] The writer disagrees because of the widely accepted interpretation that *prodere peccatorem* demands disclosure to a third party.[8] Inasmuch as there is at least doubt concerning the question, canon 2233, § 1, precludes the imposition of the penalties enacted in canon 2369, § 1, for indirect violations.

(b) To be guilty of revealing the sinner and his sin, the confessor needs to have made a disclosure of confessional information to a third party; but it is not necessary that the confessor communicates *new* knowledge to the third party. The unlawful revelation can be verified even though the third party is already aware of the same information from some other source.[9] Suppose, for example, that A, a third party, knows that B, the penitent, missed Mass on Sunday because A and B were out hunting together all that day. The confessor, who knows this sin only from confession, would be guilty of violating the seal if he were to mention to A that B did not fulfill his Sunday obligation. He would be re-

---

curreret censuram, de qua agitur."—Cappello, *Tractatus Canonico-Moralis de Censuris,* n. 193, pp. 179-180.

[7] E.g., "Poenaliter ut *indirecta* consideratur quoque violatio sigilli erga ipsum poenitentem facta."—Chelodi, *op. cit.,* n. 92, p. 137. McHugh (1880-1950)-Callan go further by stating that this could be a direct violation. Cf. *Moral Theology* (Revised by E. Farrell, 2 vols., New York: Wagner, 1958), II, n. 2768, p. 732.

[8] "Inde ultra videtur sequi, quod peracta confessione, et absolutione impensa, non possit confessor etiam in occulto exprobrare illi confitenti peccata confessa, vel eum reprehendere, nec de illis cum illo confabulari, nisi de consensu poenitentis. Ratio, quia quamvis *non sit hoc prodere, seu revelare confessionem,* est tamen eam onerosam facere et odiosam."—De Medina, *De Poenitentia, Restitutione, et Contractibus* (Ingolstadii: D. Sartorii, 1581), *De confessione,* tr. 2, *De his quae a confessore celanda sunt,* q. 47.

[9] ". . . animadvertendum est sufficere factum revelationis e notitia sacramentali, sed non requiri . . . ut agatur de revelatione stricte dicta, i.e. ut audientes hoc antea ignoraverint. . . ."—Chrétien, *De Sigillo Sacramentali,* p. 97.

vealing B's sin to A, even though A, already aware of B's sin, received no *new* knowledge of the fact.[10]

(c) For the confessor to be guilty of revealing the sinner and his sin, it is not necessary that the third party to whom the sacramental information is communicated realizes that the confessor is speaking from confessional knowledge. If the confessor is actually disclosing confessional knowledge, he violates the seal whether his listeners do or do not realize that it is such. "It is important to observe that the hearer need not know that confessional knowledge is being revealed."[11]

(d) To be guilty of betraying the sinner it is not postulated that those to whom an illicit revelation is made actually know the sinner. It is sufficient that the confessor identifies the sinner.[12]

DIRECT AND INDIRECT VIOLATIONS OF THE LAW OF CANON 889

It is the seal as defined in canon 889 that is fortified with the canonical penalties as enacted in canon 2369. These penalties vary according to whether the violation of the law of canon 889 is direct or indirect. Both direct and indirect violations concern a disclosure of the sinner and his sin. In direct violations the confessor's action in itself constitutes an actual disclosure of the

---

[10] Ojetti (1862-1932) taught otherwise concerning the pre-Code penalties for violating the seal: " 'Sacerdos, ait Innocentius III, qui peccatum in poenitentiali iudicio sibi detectum praesumpserit revelare (ergo tertiae personae illud nescienti) non solum a sacerdotali officio deponendum decernimus, verum etiam ad agendam perpetuam poenitentiam in arctum monasterium detrudendum.' "—The parentheses are his.—*Synopsis Rerum Moralium et Iuris Pontificii* (Editio tertia emendata et aucta, 3 vols., Romae: Ex Officina Polygraphica Editrice, 1909-1912), III, "Sigillum Sacramentale," n. 3736, col. 3696.

Iorio writes somewhat similarly: "Si vero audientes peccatum paenitentis iam aliunde norint, et hoc compertum sit confessario de tali peccato loquente, revelatio erit indirecta."—*Theologia Moralis,* III, n. 633, p. 364.

The writer believes this opinion carries little weight, inasmuch as all authors agree that public sins are no less guarded by the seal than occult sins.

[11] Davis, *Moral and Pastoral Theology,* III, 323.

[12] Violatio directa sigilli "committitur, etsi poenitens non sit notus audientibus, ut Gubernator Londinensis, dummodo persona designetur."—Regatillo, *Ius Sacramentarium,* n. 555, p. 321.

sinner and his sin; in indirect violations the confessor's action in itself involves a potential disclosure of the sinner and his sin.

> The seal may be violated directly or indirectly. It is violated directly when any matter of the seal is explicitly disclosed and the person of the penitent clearly designated, whether he is known to the hearers or not, whether they realize or not that the information conveyed to them was obtained through sacramental confession.
>
> There is indirect violation in the proper sense when the revelation is not intended but permitted, i.e., there is danger that the person will be known or that suspicion of his sin may result.[13]

> Sigillum *directe* laeditur, quando quis poenitentem prodit, ita quidem, ut huiusmodi proditio saltem ex fine operis directe seu in se ab eo intenta dicenda sit. Ad hoc requiritur ut et peccatum accusatum et peccator manifestentur, sive explicite sive implicite sive ex adiunctis talibus quae peccatorem reddunt certo cognoscibilem. Sigillum dicitur violari *indirecte* quando quis . . . sese exponit periculo prodendi poenitentem, quamvis id non intendat (laesio indirecta . . . sigilli stricte dicti).[14]

A direct violation, therefore, consists in this: the confessor speaks or acts in such a way that the *finis operis* of his action is a clear disclosure of the sinner and his sin. This does not mean that the confessor must advert to the fact that his action violates the seal before one can say that objectively he violates it directly. Rather, it means that the action intended and performed by him has as its *finis operis* the communication of the identity of the sinner and his sin. It is in this sense that some authors define a direct violation as one in which the betrayal of the sinner is in-

[13] Ayrinhac, *Penal Legislation in the New Code of Canon Law* (Revised by P. J. Lydon, New York: Benziger Brothers, 1936), n. 337, p. 277. "Notandum est Conc. Trevirense a. 1227 primum protulisse verbalem distinctionem inter *sigilli violationem directam et indirectam* ('Nullus sacerdos revelet confessionem directe, vel indirecte')."—Doronzo, *De Poenitentia,* II, 803.

[14] Damen in Palazzini-De Jorio, *Casus Conscientiae,* II, Casus 321, ad II, p. 230.

tended. The confessor intends an action which at least *ex fine operis* immediately discloses the sinner and his sin.[15]

In every direct violation of the seal there is a clear identification or designation of the penitent. This does not mean, however, that the penitent must be designated by name. As long as he is clearly identified, whether by name, profession, rank, time of confession, or in any other way, this suffices.

An indirect violation, on the other hand, is one which results from an action which in itself is not the disclosure of sin and sinner, but which creates a resulting danger that an awareness of, or at least a suspicion about, the sinner and his sin will ensue.[16]

Perhaps an example will clarify the distinction between a direct and indirect violation of the seal: A parish sexton tells his pastor in sacramental confession that he is the one who has been pilfering money from the poor box. Later, when police accuse an innocent youth of having robbed the poor box, the pastor in his haste to clear the youth, blurts out unthinkingly that it is not the youth but the sexton who is to blame. This would be, at least materially, a direct violation of the seal. Even though the pastor in his excitement might not have reflected on the fact that he was violating the seal, his declaration to the police is an action intended by him which has as its *finis operis* the disclosure of the youth's innocence and the sexton's guilt (sin and sinner).

On the other hand, suppose that the pastor intends to disclose nothing at all but simply dismisses the sexton from his position as a result of the confession. (The pastor's action would violate the law of canon 890, but this is not the point here.) The dismissal of the sexton is an action which in itself does not consist in the disclosure of anything. The pastor in this case does not

---

15 "Directa est laesio, si poenitentis proditio a revelante *intendatur* ut finis vel medium, proinde si simul materia sigilli reveletur et nomine, signis, variis circumstantiis, sufficienter designetur persona poenitentis, hocque in se intendatur."—Chrétien, *op. cit.*, p. 97.

16 "Indirecta est laesio, si proditio poenitentis non intendatur, sed tantum, etiam cum parva probabilitate, praevideatur secutum ex actione ad alium finem posita et nihilominus permittatur, proinde si, ex verbis, signis, factis per imprudentiam positivam prolatis, periculum quovis modo adsit simul aliis revelandi materiam sigilli et aliquam personam sufficienter designandi."—Chrétien, *op. cit.*, p. 97.

intend to communicate any knowledge of the sexton's sin to anyone. Nevertheless, if others know of the pilfered poor box and then learn of the sexton's dismissal, they may very well suspect the connection between the two. In such a case the pastor would not be guilty of directly revealing the sinner and his sin. But his action would constitute an indirect violation of the seal because of the ensuing danger of consequent revelation of, or at least suspicion about, the sinner and his sin.[17]

VIRTUES VIOLATED

Two virtues—religion and justice—demand observance of the seal of confession. Violations of the seal involve violations of one or both of these virtues.

The good or welfare of the sacrament of penance and the reverence due it call for the observance of sacramental secrecy; for this reason the seal obliges by force of the virtue of religion. Violations of the seal are always contrary to the virtue of religion.

A second basis for the seal is the virtue of justice, and this in a twofold manner, inasmuch as both natural and/or committed secrets can be involved. If the confessor's disclosure of a penitent's sin were to bring injury or defamation to the penitent's reputation, then natural secrecy would be violated and the malice of injustice would be added to the confessor's sin. In some cases, however, such detraction could not be charged against the confessor, were he to break the seal, inasmuch as the sin was already publicly known, or sufficient reasons were present to excuse from the observance of *natural* secrecy.

---

[17] Other examples of indirect violations can be listed as follows: "Indirectam sed stricte acceptam violationem sigilli committit confessarius:—a) qui non a primo confessionis initio, sed cum *producta* iam est, *paenitenti surdo dicat alta voce*: *'Redi' vel 'Quotiens'*;—b) qui sedens in confessionali, assurgat et modo quem *astantes observare* possunt legat tabulam *casuum* reservatorum;—c) *qui gestu visibili,* vel *gemitu manifestet mirationem vel tristitiam;*—d) qui, audita confessione extemplo ab ecclesia discedat, nihil sollicitus de paenitentis communione, *quae, ante confessionem, veri similis* videbatur;—e) qui ex duobus paenitentibus, v.g. duobus fratribus, *alterum solum laudat,* vel dicit, *ab eo sola* venialia afferri. De altero enim suspicionem materiae seriae, vel gravis peccati, vel indispositionis ingerit."—Vermeersch, *Theologia Moralis,* III, n. 471, p. 302.

In addition to the natural secret, there is also the question of the committed secret. The penitent must be considered as confessing his sins with the understanding that they will not be manifested to anyone. An implicit contract between penitent and confessor binds the latter not to reveal the committed or entrusted secret. Regarding this contractual or committed secrecy, some authors maintain that violations of the seal would not in every case necessarily involve the injustice of betraying an entrusted secret. Sufficient reasons could be present in an individual case to excuse one from honoring the agreement or contract by which the secret received the title of committed or entrusted. This would be verified, for example, in a case wherein the common good would call for the disclosure of the secret if it were no more than a committed secret. It must be noted that this reasoning is not an attempt to justify violations of the seal under certain conditions. Rather, it is an attempt to show that violations of the seal in some cases, while contrary to the virtue of religion, would not contain the further malice of sins against the virtue of justice.[18]

Other authors disagree, asserting that every violation of the seal includes the injustice of betraying a committed secret.[19] Suarez held it as probable, and De Lugo as more probable, that the contract of secrecy between confessor and penitent binds the confessor in every case without exception. The penitent by an implicit pact intends to bind the confessor to the total secrecy inherent in

---

[18] E.g., Doronzo writes: ". . . virtus religionis semper influit in observatione sigilli, et ratio sacrilegii numquam abest ab eius violatione; e contra duplex iustitia non semper influit et duplex peccatum iniuriae non semper committitur, quia aliquando poenitens non habet ius ad famam, cum nempe peccatum eius est manifestum, vel non habet ius ad observantiam secreti commissi, cum nempe haec sit in damnum commune, tunc enim urget sola virtus religionis et committitur solum peccatum sacrilegii."—*De Poenitentia,* II, 840.

[19] E.g., Cappello writes: "Unde violatio sigilli duplicem malitiam, imo quandoque triplicem habet. Malitia contra religionem semper habetur; item malitia contra iustitiam propter violatum contractum tacite initum, deficiente poenitentis consensu, semper adest; malitia, e contra, contra iustitiam ob violatum secretum naturale, interdum abest, ex. gr. si peccatum, quod revelatur, iam sit publicum, ita ut poenitens nullum damnum patiatur in fama."—*Tractatus Canonico-Moralis de Sacramentis,* II, n. 584, p. 603.

the sacrament. Since no reason or necessity justifies a breaking of the seal, no reason or necessity can excuse the confessor from this pact or contract. By implicit contract the confessor agrees not to betray the penitent so long as he is not obliged to do so. And, of course, he is never obliged nor ever permitted to do so, no matter how great the reason might be. In every case, therefore, violations of the seal would, according to these authors, include the injustice of breaching a contract.[20]

PENALTIES FOR VIOLATIONS OF THE SEAL

Canon 2369 establishes penalties for those who violate the sacramental seal. The first paragraph of that canon considers the confessor-violator of the seal; the second paragraph concerns other violators. In either case the penalties apply only to violations of the seal as defined in canon 889.

One prefatory point must be noted. As previously seen, authors generally agree on the objects and subjects embraced by the seal of confession. But some questions concerning the objects and subjects of the seal are disputed. These disputed points constitute doubts of law. It is certain that probabilism cannot be used to resolve these doubts. In doubts the benefit must always favor the observance of the seal. Not to observe the seal in cases of doubt is sinful. It does not follow, however, that such non-observance would render one liable to the penalties established for violators of the seal. In doubts of law all purely ecclesiastical laws cease to bind.[21] While the due honoring of the seal is not a purely ecclesiastical law, nevertheless, the penalties for violations of the seal are of strictly ecclesiastical origin. Consequently, in doubts of law they are not applicable. Canon 2233, § 1, makes this more explicit in regard to *ferendae sententiae* penalties. On this matter, Chelodi (1880-1922) wrote as follows:

> Delictum gravissimum est *directa* sigilli *violatio* . . . ad delictum requiritur plena imputabilitas; in dubio iuris

[20] Cf. Suarez, *De Poenitentia,* disp. 33, sect. 1, n. 14; De Lugo, *De Sacramento Poenitentiae,* disp. 23, sect. 1, n. 16.

[21] Cf. c. 15.

vel facti, tum quoad elementum obiectivum, tum quoad subiectivum, favendum est reo. . . . DD. morales oppositum quidem tradunt et recte, quia ipsi de peccato praecavendo, nos de illo puniendo loquimur.[22]

Canon 2369, § 1, establishes penalties for confessors who presume to violate the seal of confession. Most of the authors agree that the term "confessor" in this canon includes also priests who hear confessions without the necessary jurisdiction. Augustine (1872-1943), however, dissented.[23] On the other hand, most of the authors agree that a layman who poses as a confessor is not included under the "confessor" mentioned in canon 2369, § 1. This is true even of those authors who include such a bogus confessor under the obligation delineated in canon 889, § 1.[24] Noldin (1838-1922) disagreed.[25] The layman who pretends to be a confessor does not seem to be included since the penalties enacted in canon 2369, § 1, for indirect violations of the seal are, for the most part, meaningless with respect to laymen.

A confessor who presumes to violate the seal directly incurs automatically an excommunication which is most specially reserved to the Holy See. This excommunication is a *latae sententiae* penalty. To incur it, however, the confessor must *presume* to violate the seal directly. Any diminution of imputability on the part either of the intellect or of the will excuses one from this

---

[22] *Ius Canonicum de Delictis et Poenis,* n. 92, p. 137 and footnote 4.

[23] Cf. *A Commentary on the New Code of Canon Law* (8 vols., vol. VIII, 3rd ed., St. Louis: B. Herder, 1931), VIII, p. 442.

[24] E.g., Conte a Coronata, while teaching that a layman who pretends to be a confessor falls under the term "confessor" in canon 889, § 1, nevertheless writes concerning canon 2369, § 1: "Confessariorum nomine hic venire videntur solum confessarii veri qui sint saltem sacredotes, licet forte ad confessiones excipiendas non approbati."—*Institutiones Iuris Canonici,* IV, n. 2148, p. 640. Cf. also *ibid.,* n. 2143, p. 632.

[25] "Confessarius autem poenae obnoxius est sive sit verus sive fictus seu per errorem existimatus, ergo etiam laicus qui se confessarium simulat vel pro confessario habetur et cui poenitens bona fide confitetur."—*De Censuris* (C.I.C. adaptavit A. Schönegger, editio C.I.C. adaptata XX, Oenlponte: F. Rauch, 1940), n. 56, p. 53.

penalty.[26] This most specially reserved excommunication applies also to the Oriental Churches.[27]

A confessor who presumes to violate the seal indirectly renders himself liable to the *ferendae sententiae* penalties enacted in canon 2368, § 1. These penalties are the ones established for priests guilty of solicitation. Accordingly, the confessor who presumes to violate the seal indirectly lays himself open to being:

(a) suspended from celebrating Mass;

(b) suspended from hearing confessions;

(c) declared incapable of hearing confessions, if the gravity of his delict calls for this declaration;

(d) deprived of all benefices, dignities, the right of active and passive voice in ecclesiastical elections;

(e) declared incapable of obtaining benefices, dignities, the right of active and passive voice in ecclesiastical elections;

(f) degraded, if the seriousness of the case warrants this.

Canon 2369, § 2, makes provision for penalizing those who violate the law of canon 889, § 2. In other words, it provides penalties for persons, other than confessors, who rashly (*temere*) violate the seal. The interpreter, the superior in reserved cases, the theologian consulted by a confessor, bystanders who overhear a confession, and all others, the confessor excepted, who are bound by the seal fall into this class if they become violators of the seal. In respect to these persons, no distinction of penalties is made on the basis of whether their violations are direct or indirect. In either case the penalties are of a *ferendae sententiae* character. Specific penalties are not established, but the penalty is to be meted out according to the gravity of each case. The canon does mention, however, that the penalty can be excommunication.

---

[26] Cf. c. 2229.

[27] Cf. Decretum S. Officii, 12 Iulii, 1934—*Acta Apostolicae Sedis,* XXVI (1934), 550.

CHAPTER VII

THE FORBIDDEN USE OF CONFESSIONAL KNOWLEDGE (CANON 890)

Canon 890 forbids any and all use of confessional knowledge *cum gravamine poenitentis*. This is true even if the use of such knowledge causes no danger whatsoever that the confession will be revealed. The first paragraph of canon 890 lays down this prohibition for all confessors; the second paragraph applies it explicitly to superiors. A brief conspectus of the historical development of canon 890 will facilitate a proper understanding of the prohibition.

HISTORICAL BACKGROUND OF CANON 890

As previously mentioned, the IV General Council of the Lateran (1215), in binding the faithful with the precept of annual confession, took occasion to legislate concerning the seal of confession.[1] This law, demanding a strict observance of the sacramental seal, was a clear enunciation of the basic obligation resting upon the confessor. "The Fourth Council of the Lateran to a certain extent brought the external development of the Seal to a close."[2] "From the days of Innocent III to our own the decree of the Lateran Council has remained the classical text on the Seal of Confession."[3] But while the Lateran Council delineated the fundamental obligation of the seal, yet it left a number of questions to be debated by theologians and canonists for many years. One of these questions concerned the lawfulness of using confessional knowledge in instances wherein such use did not betray the sinner by revealing him and his sin. More precisely, it was the use of confessional knowledge *cum gravamine poenitentis* that was questioned. The text of the Lateran Council shows that some use of confessional

---

[1] Cf. *supra*, p. 15

[2] Kurtscheid, *A History of the Seal of Confession*, p. 329.

[3] O'Donnell, "The Seal of Confession," *Irish Theological Quarterly*, VIII (1913), 31.

knowledge was allowed, for it permitted the confessor to seek another's advice when necessary, provided the penitent was in no way disclosed. But the Council did not treat the use of confessional knowledge *cum gravamine poenitentis.* In the thirteenth and subsequent centuries, authors, incorrectly, were much more liberal than canon 890 in allowing the priest to make such use of information learned in confession. Only gradually did theologians and canonists, under the guidance of ecclesiastical authority, abandon the more liberal and erroneous opinion. The question was debated principally from the time following the IV General Council of the Lateran (1215) to the pontificate of Innocent XI (1676-1689), when a decree of the Holy Office (1682) for the most part settled the issue.[4] Prior to the decree of the Holy Office, a decree issued by Pope Clement VIII in 1593 to superiors of religious orders made some inroads on the more liberal and erroneous opinion.[5]

During the centuries when the question was discussed, authors expressed their opinions in solutions for several standard cases which illustrate what is understood as *gravamen poenitentis.* The more liberal opinion ERRONEOUSLY allowed the following uses of confessional knowledge, PROVIDED such uses would in no way cause the confession to be revealed:

(a) A prior confesses to his abbot. Revealed in the confession is the fact that the penitent's office of prior involves an occasion of sin for him or detriment to the community. On the supposition that the prior refuses to resign his office, the abbot could remove him from it for the good of his soul or for the welfare of the community. Many authors added the proviso that removal from office was allowable under these circumstances provided the incumbent was removable at will.[6] But even this proviso did not save the opinion from error.

---

[4] "Doctorum enim usque ad saeculum XVI opinio fuit communis cognitionis in confessione haustae usum licere, ubi non esset ullum manifestationis peccati periculum."—Galtier, *De Paenitentia,* p. 473.

[5] Cf. *infra,* p. 91.

[6] E.g., De Soto (1494-1560) wrote: "Praeterea si provincialis novit per confessionem, Priorem, aut Guardianum in ordinibus mendicantibus, scelerosum esse perniciosum conventui: quia huiusmodi officium non est ad nutum amovibile, non potest Provincialis priorem amovere, . . . Si tamen officium

(b) If a priest knows from confession that a candidate for an office or dignity is unworthy of receiving it, the confessor not only can but should use this information in deciding to vote against the penitent. One author even contended that a confessor who voted for a candidate known from confession to be unworthy incurred the penalties established by law for those who knowingly vote for an unworthy person.[7]

(c) If a priest realizes from a penitent's confession that the latter is unworthy of receiving Holy Communion or that his contemplated marriage will be invalid because of some impediment, the confessor can and should refuse these sacraments to the penitent. A number of authors contended that a priest who was not bound by office to administer these sacraments to the party involved could refuse them even on the basis of confessional knowledge alone; he could not do so, however, if he was obliged to administer the sacraments, as, for example, in the case of a pastor of the penitent.[8] Again the proviso failed to save the opinion from error.

These typical cases illustrate the tenor of that incorrect teaching regarding the use of confessional knowledge which received widespread acceptance during the thirteenth and subsequent centuries. The proponents of this liberal and erroneous doctrine contended that for a justifying reason the confessor could use sacramental information *cum gravamine poenitentis* provided no revelation of the confession could possibly ensue. By justifying reasons they meant such reasons as the penitent's spiritual welfare or the welfare of the community.

In a few sentences De Palude (1280-1342) set down the under-

---

est ad nutum amovibile: ut si praelatus vicarium suum, aut magistrum novitiorum novit in confessione perniciosos esse, tunc potest certe, et debet illos amovere, vel dando alias causas . . . vel quia vult instituere alios, qui sunt sibi magis amici: quamvis suspicionem de se faciat acceptionis personarum."—*Liber de Tegendo et Detegendo Secreto* (Salmanticae: Excudebat Ioannes Maria a Terranova, 1566), membr. 3, q. 4, concl. 5, dub. 1.

[7] Cf. Azpilcueta (Navarrus), *De Poenitentia—Opera Omnia* (6 vols., Venetiis: Apud Ioannem Guerilium, 1618), III, dist. 6, cap. pen. Sacerdos, nn. 147-150.

[8] Cf. e.g., De Palude, *Quartus Sententiarum Liber* (Parisiis: Venundantur a Johanne Petit, 1518), dist. 21, q. 3, art. 3, concl. 3.

lying principles of this school of thought. He wrote that confession did not deprive a confessor of his rights; nor did it grant him new rights in another forum. Provided no revelation of the confession resulted, the confessor was free to do or to omit whatever he judged necessary for the penitent's welfare or for the common good. This held true even if he would have acted otherwise before hearing a confession. If, for example, an abbot knew from a prior's confession that the latter should not be in charge of the monastery, and if the prior was removable at the abbot's will, then the abbot was to wait until he could remove the subordinate from office without causing suspicion about the confession, but then was to remove him immediately. From his hearing of confessions the priest was normally obliged by no other duty than that of keeping secrecy. But if he was obliged by anything else, then that was to provide for the welfare of the penitent's soul.[9]

According to De Soto, the priest's freedom in using confessional knowledge was regulated by this principle:

> Sacerdotes, propter scientiam quam habent in confessione, non possunt postmodum privare poenitentem eo, ad quod habet quodammodo ius acquisitum: sed tamen in gratuitis, ubi habent liberam potestatem, possunt eum et privare et non admittere.[10]

Some might object, said De Soto, that such freedom in using confessional knowledge as was admitted by the liberal opinion here being considered would make men afraid to confess their sins; subjects would fear confessing to their prelates; candidates for office, to their electors, and so forth. De Soto answered that persons

---

[9] "Item confessio non aufert confessori ius suum: nec tribuit ius novum in alio foro. Quidquid ergo videtur confessori faciendum vel omittendum pro bono confitentis vel communi potest facere vel omittere: dum tamen per hoc non reveletur confessio ad quod solum obligatur: licet alias non esset illud facturus. Si ergo per confessionem prioris vel alterius scit abbas quod non expedit priori tenere monasterium et sit talis qui ad libitum alias potest amoveri: expectet quousque sine nota revelationis possit amovere: et tunc statim amoveat. Cum enim ex audientia confessionis ad nihil obligetur: nisi ad celandum: et si obligaretur ad aliquid hoc esset ad medendum animae poenitentis."—*Loc. cit.*

[10] *Op. cit.*, membr. 3, q. 4, concl. 5, dub. 1.

who dreaded confession because of this had no reason to blame either the priest or the sacrament. A confessor did not wrong a penitent by denying to the latter something to which he had no acquired or vested right.[11]

Of great importance in the defeat of the too liberal opinion regarding the use of confessional knowledge was an instruction of 1590 issued by Claudius Aquaviva (1543-1615), Fifth General of the Society of Jesus (1581-1615). This instruction strictly warned Jesuit superiors against the extra-sacramental use of confessional knowledge. "The year 1590 marks a turn in our question."[12]

Aquaviva noted the opinion of some that such a use was at times justified provided no suspicion about the confession resulted. He forbade the Society's superiors from following this opinion. Such a use of confessional knowledge not only demanded a degree of caution which it was difficult to observe, but it also limited the penitent's freedom in speaking openly to his confessor. Because of the reverence in which the Society had always held the inviolable seal and the freedom in approaching this sacrament, all superiors were diligently to be on guard lest they or any member of the Society ever introduce, teach, or apply the contrary teaching. Rather, Jesuit confessors had to act in all cases as though they had heard absolutely nothing in confession.[13]

Aquaviva's prohibition applied to the Society of Jesus. Three years later, on May 26, 1593, Pope Clement VIII in his decree, *Sanctissimus,* issued a similar prohibition for all regulars. The fourth paragraph of that decree forbade the superiors of religious orders from using confessional knowledge in the external government of the community:

> Tam Superiores pro tempore existentes, quam confessarii, qui ad superioritatis gradum fuerint promoti,

---

[11] *Loc. cit.*

[12] Kurtscheid, *A History of the Seal of Confession,* p. 212.

[13] Cf. *Institutum Societatis Iesu* (3 vols., Florentiae: Ex Typographia a SS. Conceptione, 1892-1893), III, *Instructiones ad Provinciales et Superiores Societatis,* Instructio V, p. 352.

> caveant diligentissime, ne ea notitia, quam de aliorum peccatis in confessione habuerunt, ad exteriorem gubernationem utantur.[14]

Clement's decree was later to be incorporated in canon 890, § 2, of the Code of Canon Law.

The decree of Clement VIII made inroads on the opinion which favored the use of confessional knowledge. It did not, however, completely decide the issue. The decree was addressed to superiors of religious orders. Did its prohibition extend to others? Was it a purely ecclesiastical law, or rather a clarification of the obligation imposed by the divine law? And so the debate continued.[15]

Writing after Clement VIII's decree, Sanchez (1550-1610) outlined the reasons given for and against the opinion which allowed the confessor to use confessional knowledge contrary to the will of the penitent. In contrast with the long list of names in favor of the liberal opinion, Sanchez cited only three, in addition to Clement VIII, who supported what is known today to be the true doctrine. The three were Armilla (i.e., B. Fumus + 1545), Dominic Banez (1528-1604), and Claudius Aquavina (1543-1615). Having outlined the two opposing schools of thought, Sanchez stated his own preference. In addition to its strong arguments, the liberal opinion enjoyed the support of so many authors that it merited to be regarded as a most probable opinion. But Sanchez himself preferred the contrary opinion in spite of the dearth in the number of its supporters. He espoused it because it showed greater favor to the sacrament of penance. Though he associated

---

[14] Clemens VIII, decr. *Sanctissimus,* 26 maii 1593, § 4—*Codicis Iuris Canonici Fontes* (Cura Emi Petri Card. Gasparri editi, 9 vols., Romae [postea Civitate Vaticana]: Typis Polyglottis Vaticanis, 1923-1939 [Vols. VII-IX ed. cura et studio Emi Iustiniani Card. Serédi]), I, n. 177 (henceforth cited *Fontes*).

[15] "Post constitutionem Clementis (1593) usque ad decretum Innocentii (1682) plures theologi et canonistae putarunt usum scientiae sacramentalis, adhuc in supradicto casu gubernationis subditorum, esse licitum secundum se et pro secularibus atque nonnisi quoad superiores religiosos in suorum subditorum gubernatione a S. Pontifice prohibitum esse."—Doronzo, *De Poenitentia,* II, 781.

himself with the second opinion, Sanchez admitted the strong probability of the first opinion.[16]

> Although Sanchez refers to the decree of Clement VIII, he does not seem to regard it as of universal obligation, for he admits that the contrary opinion, on account of the large number of its defenders, enjoys a high degree of probability.[17]

Delrio (1551-1608) likewise considered the minority opinion, the one restricting the use of confessional knowledge, to be safer and more in keeping with the reverence due the sacrament of penance. However, the more liberal opinion had probability on its side, and in some instances demanded acceptance and application. In the mind of Delrio, the prohibition enacted by Clement VIII was a human law; on the other hand, the averting of danger from the state or from one's neighbor was sometimes demanded by the divine law. Consequently, there were undoubtedly cases in which the confessor seemed bound to use his confessional knowledge precisely for averting such danger, provided there was no violation of the seal. No human law (such as Clement's) could prohibit one from using a probable opinion if that was necessary for the prevention of some grave evil. Clement was hardly speaking of such extraordinary cases, since only most rarely could or did they occur in a religious institute.[18]

Suarez referred to the common opinion that, barring a direct or indirect revelation of the confession, the use of confessional knowledge was lawful. He did not dare to reject this opinion as wrong in itself, but he contended that it could be prohibited because of the dangers involved. "Sententiam vero communem, ex natura rei seu sola ratione spectatam, improbare non valeo; adverto autem, id, quod per se malum non est, ob periculum mali

---

[16] Cf. *Disputationum de Sancto Matrimonii Sacramento Tomi Tres* (3 vols., Antverpiae: Apud Henricum Aertssium, 1626), I, lib. 3, *De consensu clandestino,* disp. 16.

[17] Kurtscheid, *op. cit.,* p. 219.

[18] Cf. *Disquisitionum Magicarum Libri Sex* (3 vols. in 1, Moguntiae: Apud Ioannem Albinum, 1603), III, *Methodus Iudicum et Confessariorum Directioni Commoda,* lib. 6, cap. 1, sect. 2.

posse prohiberi."[19] The decree of Clement VIII for the superiors of regulars was an example of such a prohibition. In the opinion of Suarez, therefore, this decree reflected merely human law. The same opinion was held by others, such as Sylvius (1581-1649) and Tanner (1572-1632).[20]

The decree of Clement VIII was reaffirmed by two Sacred Congregations. After consultation with Pope Urban VIII and in virtue of a special faculty granted by him, the Sacred Congregation of the Council in 1624 issued a decree which reaffirmed Clement VIII's constitutions and decrees pertaining to religious orders. Their provisions were to be observed strictly.[21] In 1627, the Sacred Congregation of Bishops and Regulars warned a religious superior to exercise great caution and circumspection in processing reserved cases. In conformity with the decree of Clement VIII, knowledge derived from handling reserved cases was not to be used in the external governing of subjects.[22]

While the decree of Clement VIII was considered by a number of authors to be a purely human prohibition, yet the opinion which opposed the use of confessional knowledge *cum gravamine poenitentis* gained additional supporters. Laymann (1594-1635), for example, defended the view that confessional knowledge could not be used in external government, in the administration of the sacraments, and the like. In these matters the priest could not do what otherwise he would not have done, nor could he omit what otherwise he would have done, if he had not heard the confession of the party concerned. Otherwise the penitent would often suspect that his confession was the basis for this or that action on the part of the confessor. And even if the penitent did not have such suspicions, yet, if the faithful knew that such information could be used against them, they would feel repelled from confession. It

---

[19] *De Poenitentia,* disp. 33, sect. 7.

[20] Cf. Sylvius, *Commentaria in Supplementum sive Additiones ad Tertiam Partem D. Thom. Aquinatis* (Duaci: Sumptibus Marci Wyon, 1622), q. 11, *De Sigillo Confessionis,* art. 1, quaeritur 3; Tanner, *Theologia Scholastica* (4 vols., Ingolstadii: Impensis Ioannis Bayr, Typis Guilhelmi Ederi, 1626-1627), IV, *De Poenitentia,* disp. 6, q. 9, dub. 6, n. 143.

[21] S.C.C., decr. 21 Sept. 1624, § 1—*Fontes,* n. 2454.

[22] S. C. Ep. et Reg., *Aversana,* 30 apr. 1627—*Fontes,* n. 1726.

was true that the principal obligation of the seal was that of keeping the confession hidden and secret. But this was not the sole obligation, as some authors contended. The confessor was also obliged not to use confessional knowledge in a way that would prove burdensome to the penitent and perhaps would even deter him from the sacrament.[23] The same opinion was held by other authors, such as Bonacina (ca. 1585-1631) and Castropalao (1581-1633), who cited Clement VIII's decree in support of their teaching.[24]

De Lugo must be mentioned as outstanding among the defenders of the stricter and only tenable opinion. "The most determined opponent of the laxer opinion was Cardinal De Lugo."[25] De Lugo lent his full support to the opinion which denied the confessor's right to use confessional knowledge *cum gravamine poenitentis*. In its favor he cited the decrees of Claudius Aquaviva and Clement VIII. De Lugo did not see how the contrary opinion could still be upheld in view of Pope Clement's decree. Even though it had been addressed to the superiors of regulars, yet this decree contained a universal doctrine applicable also to secular confessors. De Lugo disagreed with Suarez' contention that the first opinion should be regarded as untenable, not of its very nature but only because of the issued papal prohibition which looked to the dangers involved. For if such a use of confessional knowledge had been lawful in itself, then the pope could not have forbidden it completely to any specific group. If it had been lawful in itself, then the natural law would have demanded its use in some instances, e.g., in order to bar the electing of an unworthy person to a prelacy. A purely ecclesiastical law could not forbid the use of confessional knowledge in cases wherein the obligations of charity would call for such a use. The use of confessional knowledge,

---

[23] Cf. *Theologia Moralis* (Venetiis: Typis Georgii Valentini, 1630), lib. 5, tr. 6, cap. 14, nn. 22-23.

[24] Cf. Bonacina, *De Sacramento Poenitentiae—Opera Omnia* (3 vols., Venetiis: Sumptibus Societatis, 1687), I, disp. 5, q. 6, sect. 5, punct. 4, n. 8; Castropalao, *Operis Moralis Pars Quarta* (Editio secunda, Lugduni: Sumptibus Ioan. Bapt. Devenet, 1649), tr. 23, punct. 19, nn. 19-20.

[25] Kurtscheid, *A History of the Seal of Confession*, p. 225.

therefore, had to be regarded as prohibited by more than a purely ecclesiastical law.[26]

De Lugo formulated a rule for determining whether a particular use of confessional knowledge was contrary to the seal:

> In iis ergo, per quae confessio non revelatur, regula tota ad cognoscendum, an sint, vel non sint contra sigillum, debet esse difficultas confessionis quae proveniret ex eo, quod talis usus, vel tale genus actionum licitum esset absque poenitentis facultate.[27]

Finally, a decree of the Holy Office in 1682 was the *coup de grâce* ending the debate. During the pontificate of Innocent XI (1676-1689), a proposition concerning the use of confessional knowledge was submitted to the Holy Office. Precluding every direct or indirect revelation of confession, the proposition vindicated for the confessor the right to use confessional information to the detriment of the penitent, provided its non-use did result in an even greater detriment or evil.

> By this greater evil the advocates of the said view ordinarily understood the spiritual injury which the penitent would suffer, e.g., if a priest would give communion to an unworthy person, or a superior would not remove the occasion of sin from his subordinate. Hence the point at issue is precisely the same as that with which we have been acquainted. For the theologians quoted above considered the use of knowledge derived from confession lawful only when there was a sufficient reason for it, and this reason was above all to shield the penitent and others from serious injury.[28]

The proposition was rejected by the Holy Office:

> De propositione: "Scientia ex confessione acquisita uti licet, modo fiat sine directa aut indirecta revelatione et gravamine poenitentis, nisi aliud multo gravius ex non usu sequatur, in cuius comparatione prius merito con-

---

[26] Cf. *De Sacramento Poenitentiae,* disp. 23, sect. 5, nn. 92-98.

[27] *Ibid.,* n. 103.

[28] Kurtscheid, *op. cit.,* p. 230.

> temnatur," addita deinde explicatione sive limitatione, quod sit intelligenda de usu scientiae ex confessione acquisitae *cum gravamine poenitentis*, seclusa quacumque revelatione, atque in casu, quo multo maius gravamen eiusdem poenitentis ex non usu sequeretur.
>
> *Statutum est*: "Dictam propositionem, quatenus admittit usum dictae scientiae cum gravamine poenitentis, omnino prohibendam esse, etiam cum dicta explicatione sive limitatione."[29]

With this decree the Holy Office interdicted any and all use of confessional knowledge *cum gravamine poenitentis*. "One result of this decision of the Holy Office was that the contrary opinion of certain canonists and theologians was altogether abandoned."[30] For the most part, this decree settled the issue and ended the debate.[31] It was incorporated in canon 890, § 1, of the Code of Canon Law.

CANON 890, § 1

Canon 890, § 1, is a reiteration of the prohibition stated in the above mentioned decree of the Holy Office under Pope Innocent XI. Canon 890, § 1, therefore, is in no way an innovation.[32] It forbids any and all use of confessional knowledge *cum gravamine poenitentis*. This is true even in cases wherein no revelation of the confession would result from such a use.

This prohibition is not a purely ecclesiastical law; it is based on the divine law. As De Lugo pointed out, if it were not based on the divine law, then the Holy Father could not entirely forbid the use of confessional knowledge *cum gravamine poenitentis*, inasmuch as the natural law and also specific obligations of charity, could at times demand such a use in protection, for example, of

---

[29] S. C. C. Off., decr. 18 nov. 1682—*Fontes*, n. 758.

[30] Kurtscheid, *op. cit.*, p. 232.

[31] Cf. Doronzo, *De Poenitentia*, II, 783.

[32] "Can. 890, § 1, nihil *novi* statuit, sed catholicam doctrinam enuntiat, quae iam antea certa erat ex prop. damnata ab Innocentio XI per decr. *S. Officii*, 18 nov. 1682."—Cappello, *Tractatus Canonico-Moralis de Sacramentis*, II, n. 614, p. 631.

the penitent against some grave spiritual harm, or for some other weighty reason.[33]

If a confessor by his words or actions were to reveal a confession, this would certainly, in a general sense, be a use of confessional knowledge to the detriment of the penitent. But in its technical meaning, the forbidden use of confessional knowledge prescinds from the presence or absence of revelation. The revelation of a confession causes a *gravamen;* but the forbidden use of confessional knowledge implies a *gravamen* distinct from that which is contained in the revelation of a confession.[34] It is an action detrimental to the penitent, even though no revelation of the penitent's confession ensues from it.[35]

By one and the same action, however, the confessor could make forbidden use of confessional knowledge and at the same time cause the confession to be revealed.

Furthermore, the forbidden use of confessional knowledge basically prescinds from the penitent's awareness or lack of awareness that the confessor is employing against him information gained from his confession. If the penitent realizes the connection between his own confession and the detrimental action on the part of the confessor, then, in a sense, the confessor is indirectly speaking to him about or reminding him of his sins outside of confession. But the confessor's action can be contrary to canon 890 even if the penitent does not suspect this connection. If a confessor allows confessional knowledge to give motivation for extra-sacramental

---

[33] Cf. *supra*, p. 95.

[34] Canon 890, § 1, adds the qualification *"excluso etiam quovis revelationis periculo."*

[35] "Igitur in primis cavendum est, ne usus notitiae confessionis cum revelatione directa, vel indirecta confessionis, verbis, aut factis, aut omissione, aut aliquo alio modo facta, confundatur; tunc enim incassum de eo mentio specialis fieret. Proinde advertendum est, quod omnis revelatio confessionis est usus notitiae confessionis, sed e contra non omnis usus confessionis est revelatio ejusdem, imo in re praesenti haec est hujus usus specifica natura et definitio, quod sit *violatio sigilli extra revelationem confessionis.* Inter revelationem et usum attente distinguendum est, quia illa numquam licet, iste vero licet, quando in gravamen poenitentis, vel Sacramenti non redundet."—P. Rota, *Enchiridion Confessarii et Judicis Ecclesiastici,* pars. 1, sect. 1, cap. 5, n. 49.

actions which are in any way detrimental or displeasing to the penitent, he violates canon 890, even though the penitent is unaware of the motivation or of the action itself.

In summary, one and the same action or omission on the part of the confessor could possibly:

(a) Reveal the penitent's confession;

and/or

(b) Remind the penitent of his confession or sins;

and/or

(c) Cause other detriment or disadvantage to the penitent.[86]

EXAMPLE: Peter Penitent confessed before morning Mass, but could not be absolved because of his unwillingness to abandon an occasion of sin. During the Mass, Peter approached the altar rail to receive Holy Communion. Knowing from confession that Peter was refused absolution, the confessor-celebrant by-passed Peter at the Communion rail. As a result: (a) other communicants, who saw Peter leave the confessional before Mass, suspect that something went amiss in Peter's confession (INDIRECT REVELATION OF CONFESSION); (b) Peter suffers shame at being reminded of his lack of amendment (INDIRECT SPEAKING TO THE PENITENT OUTSIDE CONFESSION); (c) Peter is denied Holy Communion solely because of his confession (*GRAVAMEN POENITENTIS*).

In the submitted example all three possible consequences resulted from the same action, or, rather, the one omission on the part of the confessor. However, any use of confessional knowledge is forbidden if (c) alone results from it, even though (a) and (b) do not also follow as a consequence.

EXAMPLE: The pastor has decided in his own mind to appoint Simon as head usher, but has informed no one of this selection. Then Simon tells the pastor in confession that he is guilty of theft. On the basis of this confessional knowledge alone, the pastor

86 "Pro quo adverte, usum illius scientiae posse esse vel cum revelatione directa, aut indirecta peccati, et tunc non est dubium quod sit contra sigillum; vel posse esse absque revelatione, sed tamen ita ut poenitens advertat id fieri propter peccatum quod confessus est: vel denique ita, ut neque ipse poenitens hoc advertat."—De Lugo, *De Sacramento Poenitentiae,* disp. 23, sect. 5, n. 102.

decides that Simon cannot be trusted to be head usher. Another person is selected for the position. The pastor's action constitutes a forbidden use of confessional knowledge, even though he in no way creates danger of a revelation of the confession or causes Simon to suspect the influence of his confession on the appointment of the head usher.

The divine law and the canon law forbid the use of confessional knowledge *cum gravamine poenitentis. Gravamen poenitentis* is a broad term embracing anything that would in any way be detrimental, disadvantageous, or displeasing to the penitent, whether in the spiritual or in the temporal order. It includes such things as embarrassment for the penitent, refusal of the sacraments, removal from office, denial of a vote in an election, aloofness or coldness towards him on the part of the confessor, and so forth.

> *Gravamen,* literally, means heaviness; metaphorically trouble or complaint, either in the spiritual or the material life.[37]

> Gravamen autem intellegendum est vel quod paenitens re vera formaliter experiatur vel quod *conaturaliter* experiretur si novisset usum istum scientiae esse factum.[38]

> What do we mean by the words "harm or displeasure?" We mean injury either in body, in soul, or in external possessions. We mean whatever would redound to the dishonor or discredit of the penitent; whatever would inconvenience him or annoy, shame, or sadden him. We mean, in a word, whatever would make the penitent even slightly regret his confession.[39]

The use of confessional knowledge is forbidden whenever it results in a *gravamen* for the penitent, even though its use would prevent a greater *gravamen*. Such a use is wrong in itself and one cannot justify it even for the sake of preventing greater detriment to the penitent. For example, if a priest knows from confession that a certain penitent's contemplated marriage will be invalid because of some impediment, the priest cannot act on the basis of

---

[37] Augustine, *A Commentary on the New Code of Canon Law,* IV, p. 304.

[38] Vermeersch-Creusen, *Epitome Iuris Canonici* (3 vols., Vol. II, 6. ed., Romae: H. Dessain, 1940), II, n. 168, p. 115.

[39] Healy, "The Seal of Confession," *Review for Religious,* II (1943), 182.

this sacramental knowledge to prevent the marriage which the penitent intends in spite of the impediment. This is true even though by using the knowledge the confessor would be able to prevent greater detriment to the penitent, namely, an unlawful and invalid marriage.[40] If the confessor were allowed to use sacramental knowledge to the detriment of the penitent in order to prevent a greater detriment, the result eventually would be an even far greater evil, namely, rendering the sacrament of penance odious.

The penitent has a right to expect the confessor not to use confessional information against him sacramentally. This right must be safeguarded, even though the penitent is unwise or unreasonable in his evaluation of detriment or disadvantage.

> The penitent may be unreasonable in judging as a hardship [*gravamen*] some occurrence which actually tends to his spiritual welfare, such as an action on the part of the confessor that would prevent him from committing sin; yet, even in this event the confessor is bound to abstain from such an action.[41]

It must be emphasized that an action (or omission) can constitute a forbidden use of sacramental information even though the penitent is unaware either of the action itself or of the link

[40] This is clear from the decree of the Holy Office in 1682 as quoted above, p. 96. "Evidenter patet ex hoc Decreto, quod prohibetur et illicitum declaratur uti quavis scientia ex confessione acquisita, si adest gravamen poenitentis, etiamsi ex non usu maius gravamen sequeretur, et recte hoc prohibetur; gravamen enim, quod ex usu provenit, etsi minus sit, ex directa et positiva confessarii opera provenit; quod autem ex non usu provenit, quamvis maius sit, tamen a confessario non provenit, nisi indirecte et permissive, et proinde ei imputari nequit, illud enim tollere, nec potest, nec debet, cum non sint facienda mala, ut eveniant bona."—P. Rota, *op. cit.*, pars 1, sect. 1, cap. 5, n. 52.

[41] Connell, *Father Connell Answers Moral Questions* (Edited by E. J. Weitzel, Washington, D. C.: The Catholic University of America Press, 1959), Q. 140, p. 136. "Quare corrigendum est hoc antiquorum principium: licet uti scientia confessionis, quando poenitens non potest esse *rationabiliter invitus* e.g. quando usus scientiae sacramentalis necessarius est ad poenitentem a peccato removendum."—Noldin-Schmitt, *Summa Theologiae Moralis,* III, n. 417, p. 429, footnote 1.

between it and his confession. To be forbidden, it suffices that an action be of a kind to which penitents would object if they realized that it could be based on confessional knowledge. If penitents in general knew even theoretically that such and such a type of detrimental action could result from their confessions, they would fear the sacrament of penance and feel repelled from it. This consequence would follow even if in practice they were unable to detect when such a use of confessional information was being made.[42]

Some specific examples of how the confessor may not employ confessional knowledge will illustrate the prohibition enacted in canon 890:

(a) A confessor may not refuse Holy Communion to a penitent because of his confessional awareness that the latter had to be refused sacramental absolution. This is true even if the penitent seeks Holy Communion in private.

(b) A confessor may not refuse his assistance at a marriage because he is aware from the parties' confessions that the marriage in question will be invalid.

(c) A confessor may not change his vote in an election on the grounds that he knows from the candidate's confession that the latter is unworthy of being elected.

(d) A parish priest may not dismiss an employee because he knows from confession of the latter's dishonesty.

(e) A confessor may not become less cordial towards an acquaintance because of something the latter discloses in confession.

(f) A confessor may not attempt to avoid hearing a certain person's confession because, for instance, he knows from previous confessions of the penitent's lack of proper dispositions required for absolution.

---

[42] "Pro quo adverte, usum illius scientiae posse esse . . . ita, ut neque poenitens hoc [id fieri propter peccatum quod confessus est] advertat. Si fiat hoc . . . modo, et non in praeiudicium ullum poenitentis; sed ita, ut etiamsi poenitens sciat, licitum esse talem usum, non ideo retardetur a confessione; tunc non videtur esse ullo modo contra sigillum, aut contra sacramentum: si vero esset ille usus gravis poenitenti, atque ideo difficilius confiteretur, si sciret, illum usum esse licitum; tunc usus erit illicitus."—De Lugo, *De Sacramento Poenitentiae,* disp. 23, sect. 5, n. 102.

It goes without saying that these examples can be multiplied indefinitely.

A pertinent and interesting question is this: Would a confessor violate the law either of canon 889 or of canon 890 by endeavoring to discover the identity of his penitent, for example, by peering through the curtain as the penitent departs from the confessional? Of the authors who treat the question, a number state that such an action is not contrary to the seal. Of these authors, one calls the action reprehensible, and another, a sin of curiosity.[43] At least one author considers it a forbidden use of confessional knowledge.[44]

Not all uses of confessional knowledge are forbidden to the confessor by canon 890, but only those uses which entail a *gravamen* for the penitent. Consequently, as a result of hearing confessions, the confessor may, for example, pray for a particular penitent; he may consult books about a confessional problem; he may strive more earnestly to overcome his own faults; he may

---

[43] "Sigillum obligat confessarium erga alios tantum, non autem *erga semetipsum*: hinc reprehensione quidem dignus est, at non agit contra sigillum confessarius, qui absque ratione sufficiente res in confessione auditas apud semetipsum recogitet,—qui ad cognoscendos poenitentes oculos ex confessionali in eos coniiciat,—qui alios de nomine poenitentium suorum qua talium interrogat, nisi alii ex hac sua agendi ratione rem gravem de poenitente suspicentur."—Noldin-Schmitt, *op. cit.,* III, n. 407, p. 419.

"*Nec usus scientiae habetur,* ubi scientia est mere occasio. Quare curiositate non autem sacrilegio peccabit qui, post auditas confessiones, interroget aedituum de nomine personae quae ad confitendum accessit, nisi inde suspicio cuiusdem gravis peccati oriri facile possit."—Vermeersch, *Theologia Moralis,* III, n. 478, p. 305. Cf. also Sartori in Palazzini-De Jorio, *Casus Conscientiae,* II, Casus 434, ad I, p. 567.

[44] ". . . it is possible that in certain cases a confessor might be inclined, because of sins confessed, to take some extraordinary means to identify the penitent, for example, by looking out as the penitent leaves the confessional. Noldin calls such conduct reprehensible, but adds that it would not be a violation of the seal. I think that he means it is not a violation of the seal in the strict sense—that is, not a direct or an indirect violation. But it seems to me an illicit use of confessional knowledge; for penitents are usually helped by the opportunity to remain unknown and they would resent it if they thought that a priest would make some special attempt to identify them merely because of some sins they had confessed."—Kelly, *The Good Confessor,* p. 45.

use his confessional experience to become a better confessor, and so forth.

Many authors teach that a confessor may show greater kindness, understanding, or patience towards a penitent outside of confession because of confessional knowledge.[45] They claim this to be true even if the penitent realizes that the confessor's more benign attitude towards him is a consequence of his confession.[46] However, other authors warn that often the penitent prefers not to be reminded of his confession even by actions on the part of the confessor which in themselves are favorable to the penitent.

> Authors usually say that a priest may treat his penitents more kindly because of his confessional knowledge. They allow this, even though the penitent himself might realize that confessional knowledge is the basis for the kindness, provided, of course, that others will not be led to suspect the penitent. Personally, I think that this opinion should be applied with the greatest caution. It seems to me that, except in those circumstances in which it is perfectly clear that the penitent wishes us to use confessional knowledge for his own encouragement, it is safest to follow the first rule: namely, simply act as if the confession had not been heard. This is the best way of avoiding embarrassment and offense.[47]

CANON 890, § 2

The second paragraph of canon 890 is an explicit application to superiors of the general prohibition enunciated in the preceding paragraph of the canon.[48] It forbids present superiors as well as confessors who at some future time will be superiors from in any

---

[45] "A priest may show greater kindness and consideration for a penitent who he knows from confession is severely afflicted, provided of course the confessor's way of acting would not engender suspicion in the minds of observers."—Healy, "The Seal of Confession," *Review for Religious,* II (1943), 186.

[46] Cf. Noldin-Schmitt, *op. cit.,* III, n. 417, p. 430.

[47] Kelly, *op. cit.,* pp. 45-46. Cf. also Doronzo, *De Poenitentia,* II, 841-842.

[48] "Vetitus usus scientiae sacramentalis in iis quae ad gubernationem exteriorem spectant, de quo in can. 890, § 2, non est nisi corollarium sponte profluens ex principio generali statuto in § 1 eiusdem canonicis."—Cappello, *Tractatus Canonico-Moralis de Sacramentis,* II, n. 614, p. 632.

way employing in external government their confessional knowledge of sins. It is an incorporation into the Code of the decree *Sanctissimus* issued by Pope Clement VIII in 1593.[49] The wording of canon 890, § 2, closely resembles that of the decree. However, whereas the decree was directed to superiors of regulars, canon 890, § 2, applies to all superiors.[50]

For a confessor who is or who later becomes a superior to employ confessional knowledge in external government is something which of its nature would be odious to the penitent-inferior. The rule, therefore, is that such a use of confessional knowledge is forbidden to all superiors, present or future. Cappello notes, however, that if a particular action on the part of the superior would *certainly* not be distasteful to penitents, then it is not *in itself* unlawful.[51] If, for example, a superior learned from hearing confessions that his own excessive rigor or niggardliness was the cause of detractions or complaints among his subjects, he could consequently be more temperate or generous and thereby improve the spirit of the community. This presupposes, of course, that he would do so in such a way as not to provoke suspicions about the confessions he had heard.[52]

NO PENALTY

In the writer's opinion, as expressed in the previous chapter, the penalties enacted in canon 2369, § 1, for indirect violations of

---

[49] Cf. *supra*, p. 91.

[50] "Note that our canon speaks of *superiors generally,* though the decree of Clement VIII was intended chiefly for religious superiors. The Code therefore includes *all* superiors, whether they are already in office or to be afterwards elected. Hence bishops, religious superiors, directors of seminaries and colleges, vicars general, and all those who are employed by the Roman Congregations are included."—Augustine, *op. cit.*, IV, 304-305.

[51] "Si gravamen poenitentis *certo* abesset, usus scientiae sacramentalis *per se* non foret illicitus."—*Op. cit.*, II, n. 623, p. 645.

[52] "Quinimo, ut observat Lugo, nec illicitus est quilibet usus huius notitiae etiam ad gubernandum. Sic si Praelatus ex confessione sciat detractiones et querelas subditorum contra illum propter nimium rigorem vel parsimoniam aut parcitatem; poterit discere, non expedire morem illum, sed indigere moderatione vel mutatione."—Ballerini-Palmieri, *Opus Theologicum Morale,* V, n. 1008.

the seal are not applicable to violations of the law enacted in canon 890.[53] The Code establishes no penalties for violations of the law which is contained in canon 890.[54]

---

[53] Cf. *supra*, p. 75.

[54] ". . . in iure poenali, usus scientiae ex confessione acquisitae cum gravamine poenitentis, excluso quovis revelationis periculo, licet severissime prohibeatur, delictum constituere non videtur, nisi ad normam can. 2222, § 1, seu, nisi quatenus usus huius scientiae scandalum praebeat aut specialem gravitatem induat, ut si Superior in sua gubernatione notitiis ex confessione acquisitis non solum utatur, sed etiam glorietur se illis uti, aut ita aperte utatur ut de hoc usu illicito sermo passim fiat inter fideles sibi subiectos."—Conte a Coronata, *Institutiones Iuris Canonici,* IV, n. 2144, p. 635.

CONCLUSIONS

1. The sacramental seal as derived from divine law, that is, the divine seal, forbids:

(a) the revelation to a third party of anything disclosed in sacramental confession, the revelation of which would be displeasing and odious to penitents (above all else, this includes the betrayal of the sinner by revealing his identity and his sin);

(b) the confessor's speaking to the penitent outside confession about confessional matter;

(c) any other use of confessional knowledge if such use would be displeasing, disadvantageous, or detrimental to the penitent. (Cf. pp. 1-5.)

2. The seal as defined in the *Code of Canon Law,* that is, the canonical seal, forbids the *proditio peccatoris.* The notion of *proditio peccatoris* is in great measure based on the decree *Omnis utriusque sexus* of the IV General Council of the Lateran. The canonical seal is defined as the obligation not to betray the sinner by revealing to a third party in a conjunctive way both the identity of the sinner and the sin he confessed. (Cf. pp. 15-23.)

3. The IV General Council of the Lateran enunciated the basic obligation of sacramental secrecy—the *non-proditio peccatoris.* It was only after this Council that theologians intensively developed the more intimate questions concerning sacramental secrecy, such as the full extent of the matter protected against revelation. While the theologians undoubtedly received impetus from the decree of the Lateran Council, the writer believes that, in determining the matter which falls under sacramental secrecy and can never be revealed, they used as their yardstick the divine seal, which is broader than the *non-proditio peccatoris* of the canonical seal. (Cf. pp. 45-48.)

4. It is for violations of the canonical seal that one becomes subject to the canonical penalties enacted in canon 2369. For such a violation it is postulated that the disclosure by the confessor be made to a third party. (Cf. pp. 75-79.)

5. The divine seal forbids the confessor to speak of confessional matters to the penitent outside of confession. To do so, however, would not constitute a violation of the canonical seal (*proditio peccatoris*) and would not render the confessor liable to the penalties enacted in canon 2369. (Cf. pp. 77-78.)

6. The divine seal forbids the confessor to use confessional knowledge if, even apart from any danger of revealing the confession, such use would cause detriment, disadvantage, or displeasure to the penitent (*cum gravamine poenitentis*). If the confessor were to do so, he would violate the divine law and canon 890, but not the canonical seal to which canon 889 adverts. Consequently, his illicit use of confessional knowledge would not subject him to the penalties enacted in canon 2369. (Cf. pp. 97-106.)

APPENDIX I

TEXTS OF CANONS

The canons dealing with the sacramental seal which were referred to in this dissertation are as follows:

CANON 889.—§ 1. Sacramentale sigillum inviolabile est; quare caveat diligenter confessarius ne verbo aut signo aut alio quovis modo et quavis de causa prodat aliquatenus peccatorem.

§ 2. Obligatione servandi sacramentale sigillum tenentur quoque interpres aliique omnes ad quos notitia confessionis quoquo modo pervenerit.

CANON 890.—§ 1. Omnino prohibitus est confessario usus scientiae ex confessione acquisitae cum gravamine poenitentis, excluso etiam quovis revelationis periculo.

§ 2. Tam Superiores pro tempore exsistentes, quam confessarii qui postea Superiores fuerint renuntiati, notitia quam de peccatis in confessione habuerint, ad exteriorem gubernationem nullo modo uti possunt.

CANON 900.—Quaevis reservatio omni vi caret:

2°. Quoties . . . prudenti confessarii iudicio, absolvendi facultas a legitimo Superiore peti nequeat sine gravi poenitentis incommodo aut sine periculo violationis sigilli sacramentalis.

CANON 1757.—§ 3. Ut incapaces (repelluntur a testimonio ferendo):

2°. Sacerdotes, quod attinet ad ea omnia quae ipsis ex confessione sacramentali innotuerunt, etsi a vinculo sigilli soluti sint; imo audita a quovis et quoquo modo occasione confessionis ne ut indicium quidem veritatis recipi possunt.

CANON 2027.—§ 2. Admitti nequeunt (ut testes):

1°. Confessarius ad normam can. 1757, § 3, n. 2.

CANON 2369.—§ 1. Confessarium, qui sigillum sacramentale directe violare praesumpserit, manet excommunicatio specialissimo modo Sedi Apostolicae reservata; qui vero indirecte tantum, obnoxius est poenis do quibus in can. 2368, § 1.

§ 2. Quicunque praescriptum can. 889, § 2 temere violaverit, pro reatus gravitate plectatur salutari poena, quae potest esse etiam excommunicatio.

APPENDIX II

Instruction of the Holy Office, June 9, 1915[1]

An Instruction of the Holy Office, sent to the Ordinaries of places and to the General Superiors of religious Orders, is as follows:

> That the natural and divine law of the sacramental seal has always and everywhere in the Church of Christ been most faithfully kept, not even the bitterest enemies of sacramental confession have ever been able seriously to question. And beyond a doubt this is to be attributed to the most provident design of the Almighty, who, in mercifully offering sacramental confession to men as a "second plank of salvation after the shipwreck of the loss of grace," has deigned to keep far from it every ground of offense.
>
> Yet there are sometimes found ministers of this salutary sacrament who, though they keep silence about anything that might in any way betray the person of the penitent, yet are not ashamed rashly to speak, in private conversation or in public sermons, for the edification of their hearers, as they say, of matters which have been submitted to the power of the keys in sacramental confession. Now, since in a matter of such gravity and importance not only a perfect and consummated injury but every appearance and suspicion of injury must be studiously avoided, everyone must see how thoroughly such a practice is to be condemned. For, even though it be done without substantial violation of the sacramental secret, it cannot fail to offend the ears of pious listeners and to produce in their hearts uneasiness and diminished confidence—a thing which is surely entirely foreign to the nature of this sacrament, through which the most merciful Lord, *by the pardon of His loving mercy, entirely wipes away* and quite forgets *the sins which through human weakness we have committed.*
>
> In consideration of these facts, this Supreme Sacred Congregation of the Holy Office deems it its duty to give to all Ordinaries of places and Superiors of regular Orders and of all religious institutes, a command in the Lord, gravely binding in conscience, that if they find such abuses anywhere, they take measures promptly and efficaciously to repress them; and that in future, not only in theological classes but also in conferences on moral "cases" as they are called, and in public and private talks and exhortations to the clergy, they carefully see to it that the priests subject to them be taught never to dare mention anything which pertains to the matter of sacramental confession in any form or under any pretext, especially on the occasion of sacred missions or spiritual exercises, nor even incidentally, directly or indirectly, in public or private speech (excepting the case of necessary consultation to be made according

[1] Text in translation taken from Bouscaren, *The Canon Law Digest,* I, 413-414.

to the rules laid down by approved authors); and that they give orders that their subjects be examined specially in this matter in the tests which are given them to determine their ability to hear confessions.

The Sacred Congregation is confident that no confessor will transgress these prescriptions. If the event prove otherwise, the aforesaid Ordinaries and Superiors must seriously warn the transgressors, punish with suitable penalties those who repeat the offense, and in more serious cases refer the matter as soon as possible to this Sacred Tribunal.

Given at Rome, from the palace of the Holy Office, on the 9th day of June, 1915.

APPENDIX III

Privileged Communications Between Confessor and Penitent

Canon 1757, § 3, 2°, of the *Code of Canon Law* absolutely disqualifies a confessor from acting as witness in an ecclesiastical court in regard to all things learned from or on the occasion of sacramental confession. This disqualification holds true even if the penitent agrees to free the confessor from his obligation to secrecy. Is the confessor provided with any similar disqualification or exemption from acting as a witness in the courts of the land? Or is there the possibility of a conflict between the confessor's inviolable obligation not to break the sacramental seal and the conceivable demands of the civil court that he do so?

Any exemption in the civil law permitting the confessor to refuse testimony in court concerning the confidences of the confessional would fall under the heading of "privileged communications."

> American and English law recognizes certain categories of confidential relations, the parties to which cannot be compelled to testify in court as to communications made in pursuance of such relations. Communications, thus protected, are said to be privileged. Common law jurisdictions are not agreed as to the number of relations entitled to this prerogative.[1]

For example, the confidences between lawyer and client enjoy the rank of privileged communications. Is the same privilege extended to the clergyman-penitent relation?

Regarding confidences between the clergyman and penitent, there seems to be no unanimity of opinions as to the extent to which the communications were privileged at English common law.

> Professor Wigmore sums up as follows: "But since the 'Restoration' and for more than two centuries of English practice, the almost unanimous opinion of judicial opinion . . . has denied the existence of the privilege . . . the privilege cannot be said to have been recognized as a rule of the common law in England." . . .
>
> However, in view of the actual language of the decided cases, it would seem that one D. M. Cloud, writing on the subject at the turn of the century, has phrased it more accurately. He said: "In England, at common law, the question remained ever in a nebulous state; it being decided at one time that such communications were privileged, at another that they were not so, and again a middle ground being adopted, it was said that, though they were acceptable as evidence if purely voluntary, yet they were highly improper if

[1] Allred, "The Confessor in Court," *The Jurist*, XIII (1953), 2-3.

coercion were employed . . . the question never received precise adjudication in England."[2]

In 1876, while delivering an opinion of the Supreme Court of the United States, Mr. Justice Field, by way of *dictum,* noted:

> It may be stated as a general principle that public policy forbids the maintenance of any suit in a court of justice, the trial of which would inevitably lead to the disclosure of matters which the law itself regards as confidential, and respecting which it will not allow the confidences to be violated. On this principle, suits cannot be maintained which require a disclosure of the confidences of the confessional, . . .[3]

In a recent case, the United States Court of Appeals for the District of Columbia Circuit ruled that an admission made by the defendant to a Lutheran minister after he had urged her to confess her sins was a privileged communication and the minister's testimony thereof was inadmissible.[4] It is of interest that, in examining the question of whether the disclosure of appellant to the minister was a confidential confession to a spiritual adviser, the Circuit Judge noted: "The answer would be clearer were the relationship of priest and penitent involved, where the priest is known to be bound to silence by the discipline and laws of his Church."[5]

The Circuit Judge, by way of additional statements, discussed the granting of the privilege to communications between clergyman and penitent. The following are excerpts from his remarks:

> It is highly probable that the priest-penitent privilege was part of the common law of England in the centuries preceding the Reformation. See the lengthy study by Nolan, "The Law of the Seal of Confession," 13 *Catholic Encyc.* 649-65. This same study demonstrates, however, that after the Reformation the privilege was by no means generally recognized, and in fact appears to have

---

[2] *Ibid.,* pp. 6-7. "It is quite clear, then, that at Common Law the sacredness and inviolability of the confessional were well secured; and that, whatever effect the legislation of the Reformation period may have had on other matters of Church discipline, this rule of the Church was confirmed and preserved intact by the Law."—Henriques, "English Law and the Seal of Confession," *Blackfriars,* XIV (1933), 269. ". . . what is needed is a clear exposition . . . that will establish that there was such a principle at common law. It has not disappeared. . . ."—Hogan, "The Secrecy of the Confessional and American Courts," *The Catholic Mind,* XLIX (1951), 419.

[3] *Totten, Administrator,* v. *United States,* 92 U. S. 105, 23 L. Ed. 605 (1876).

[4] *Mullen* v. *United States,* 105 U. S. App. D. C. 25, decided December 4, 1958; Additional Statements, January 29, 1959.

[5] *Loc. cit.*

> been abrogated or abandoned. Because of this it is said the claimed privilege was not one at common law and, therefore, if now to be recognized must be enacted into statute, which Congress has not done. However, as we shall see, recognition of the privilege in federal courts does not depend upon finding that it has either existed uniformly at common law or has been approved in terms by act of Congress. Before enlarging upon this it is worth noting that even during the post-Reformation period, when religious and political tensions largely set the pattern in such matters, judicial decisions and legal writings were not uniformly hostile to the privilege.
>
> It . . . appears that non-recognition of the privilege at certain periods in the development of the common law was inconsistent with the basic principles of the common law itself. It would be no service to the common law to perpetuate in its name a rule of evidence which is inconsistent with the . . . fundamental guides furnished by that law. And, as we have seen, the denial was never uniform or resolute, so strong were the claims of reason in support of the privilege. . . . In our own time, with its climate of religious freedom, there remains no barrier to adoption by the federal courts of a rule of evidence on this subject dictated by sound policy.
>
> Sound policy—reason and experience—concedes to religious liberty a rule of evidence that a clergyman shall not disclose in a trial the secrets of a penitent's confidential confession to him, at least absent the penitent's consent. Knowledge so acquired in the performance of a spiritual function as indicated in this case is not to be given to the whole world. . . . The rules of evidence have always been concerned not only with truth but with the manner of its ascertainment.[6]

In this country, however, the common law basis for the privilege between minister and penitent has not always been accepted. "In the absence of statute, the contention of privilege for the clergyman-penitent relation has not been well received in the United States."[7] This lack of recognition is illustrated by a case tried in New Jersey before that State enacted a statute granting the privilege. The Court of Errors and Appeals of New Jersey ruled: "No privilege of this nature existed at common law."[8]

Allred, whose detailed article on this subject has already been cited, sees the possibility of turning to the First Amendment as a source of protection for the confessor-penitent confidences:

> For a Catholic priest the secrecy of the confessional is prescribed by Canon Law. The Sacrament of Penance involves a rite of the Church. Any effort to compel its violation would appear to be a prohibition against that free exercise of religion which is guaranteed in the First Amendment. Since the Supreme Court of the United States has held the First Amendment equally applicable to the States, it would appear that any effort to make a

[6] Circuit Judge Fahy, *loc. cit.*

[7] Allred, "art. cit.," *The Jurist,* XIII (1953), 7.

[8] *State* v. *Morehous,* 117 Atlantic 296 (1922).

> priest violate the Seal of Confession might well be held to be a violation of constitutional rights, whether sought in a Federal or a State Court.[9]

In view of its tenuous basis in the common law, over thirty States have enacted statutes which recognize privileged communications between the clergyman and penitent. It is sustained also in the Manual for Courts Martial in the Armed Forces of the United States.[10]

---

[9] "Art. cit.," *The Jurist,* XIII (1953), 10-11.

[10] The texts of the statutes appear in an appendix to Allred's article, *ibid.*, 23-32.

BIBLIOGRAPHY

Sources

Acta Apostolicae Sedis, Commentarium Officiale, Romae, 1909-1928; Civitate Vaticana, 1929-

Canon Law Digest, The, 4 vols., Milwaukee: Bruce Publishing Co., Vol. I, 1934, Vol. II, 1943, Vol. III, 1954, edited by T. Lincoln Bouscaren; Vol. IV, 1958, edited by T. Lincoln Bouscaren and James I. O'Connor.

Codex Iuris Canonici Pii X Pontificis Maximi iussu digestus Benedicti Papae XV auctoritate promulgatus, Romae, 1917; Reprint, Westminster, Md.: The Newman Press, 1957.

Codicis Iuris Canonici Fontes, cura Emi Petri Card. Gasparri editi, 9 vols., Romae (postea Civitate Vaticana): Typis Polyglottis Vaticanis, 1923-1939). (Vols. VII-IX ed. cura et studio Emi Iustiniani Card. Serédi.)

Concilii Plenarii Baltimorensis II Acta et Decreta, Baltimorae: Excudebat Joannes Murphy, 1868.

Decretales D. Gregorii Papae IX, Romae, 1582.

Decretum Gratiani, emendatum et notationibus illustratum, una cum glossis, 2 vols., Romae, 1582.

Institutum Societatis Iesu, 3 vols., Florentiae: Ex Typographia a SS. Conceptione, 1892-1893.

Mansi, Joannes, *Sacrorum Conciliorum Nova et Amplissima Collectio,* 53 vols., Parisiis, 1901-1927.

Schema Codicis Iuris Canonici cum notis Petri Card. Gasparri, 4 vols. in 2, Romae: Typis Polyglottis Vaticanis, 1912-1914.

Reference Works

Abbo, John A.-Hannan, Jerome D., *The Sacred Canons,* revised edition, 2 vols., St. Louis: B. Herder, 1957.

Aertnys, Joseph, *Theologia Moralis,* accommodavit C. A. Damen, editio XVI, VIII post Codicem, 2 vols., Torino: Marietti, 1950.

Alphonsus Liguori, St., *Theologia Moralis,* editio nova a P. Leonardo Gaudé edita, 4 vols., Romae: Typographia Vaticana, 1905-1912.

Arregui, Antonius Maria, *Summarium Theologiae Moralis,* editio decima, Bilbao: El Mensajero Del Corazón De Jesús, 1927.

Augustine (Bachofen), Charles, *A Commentary on the New Code of Canon Law,* 8 vols., Vol. IV, 1920; Vol. VIII, 3. ed., 1931, St. Louis: B. Herder.

Ayrinhac, H. A., *Penal Legislation in the New Code of Canon Law,* revised by P. J. Lydon, New York: Benziger Brothers, 1936.

Azpilcueta (Navarrus), Martinus, *Opera Omnia,* 6 vols., Venetiis: Apud Ioannem Guerilium, 1618.

Ballerini, Antonius, *Opus Theologicum Morale*, absolvit et edidit Dominicus Palmieri, 7 vols., Prati: Ex Officina Libraria Giachetti, Filii et Soc., 1889-1893.

Beste, Udalricus, *Introductio in Codicem*, editio quarta, Neapoli: M. D'Auria, 1956.

Blat, Albertus, *Commentarium Textus Codicis Iuris Canonici*, 5 vols. in 7, Vol. III, editio secunda, 1924; Vol. V, 1924; Romae: Collegio Angelico.

Bonacina, Martinus, *Opera Omnia*, 3 vols., Venetiis, Sumptibus Societatis, 1687.

Bouscaren, T. Lincoln-Ellis, Adam C., *Canon Law, A Text and Commentary*, second revised edition, Milwaukee: Bruce Publishing Co., 1955.

Bucceroni, Januarius, *Institutiones Theologiae Moralis*, editio sexta, 4 vols., Romae: Ex Typographia Pontificia in Instituto Pii IX, 1914-1915.

Cappello, Felix, *Tractatus Canonico-Moralis de Censuris*, editio quarta emendata et aucta, Taurini: Marietti, 1950.

———, *Tractatus Canonico-Moralis de Sacramentis*, 5 vols., Vol. I, II, V, 6th ed.; Vols. II, IV, 3rd ed., Taurini: Marietti, 1949-1953.

Castropalao, Ferdinandus, *Operis Moralis Pars Quarta*, editio secunda, Lugduni: Sumptibus Ioan. Bapt. Devenet, 1649.

Cerato, Prosdocimus, *Censurae Vigentes Ipso Facto a Codice Iuris Canonici Excerptae*, editio secunda recognita, Patavii: Typis Seminarii, 1921.

Chelodi, Ioannes, *Ius Canonicum de Delictis et Poenis*, editio V, recognita et aucta a Pio Ciprotti, Vicenza: Società Anonima Tipografica fra Cattolici Vincentini, 1943.

Chrétien, P., *De Poenitentia*, Metis: Ex Typis "Imprimerie Lorraine," 1929.

Connell, Francis, *Father Connell Answers Moral Questions*, edited by E. J. Weitzel, Washington, D. C.: Catholic University of America Press, 1959.

Conte a. Coronata, Matthaeus, *Institutiones Iuris Canonici*, 5 vols., Vols. I-IV, editio quarta aucta et emendata; Vol. V, ed. 3., Taurini: Marietti, 1950-1955.

D'Annibale, Joseph, *Summula Theologiae Moralis*, editio quinta, 3 vols., Romae: Desclée, Lefebvre et Soc., 1908.

Davis, Henry, *Moral and Pastoral Theology*, fifth edition revised and enlarged, 4 vols., New York: Sheed and Ward, 1946.

Della Rocca, Fernando, *Manual of Canon Law*, tr. by A. Thatcher, Milwaukee: Bruce Publishing Co., 1959.

Delrio, Martinus, *Disquisitionum Magicarum Libri Sex*, 3 vols. in 1, Moguntiae: Apud Ioannem Albinum, 1603.

De Lugo, Joannes, *Disputationes Scholasticae et Morales*, editio nova, 8 vols., Parisiis: Apud Ludovicum Vivès, 1868-1869.

De Medina, Joannes, *De Poenitentia, Restitutione, et Contractibus*, Ingolstadii: D. Sartorii, 1581.

De Meester, Alphonsus, *Iuris Canonici et Iuris Canonico-Civilis Compendium*, nova editio ad normam C.I.C., 3 vols. in 4, Brugis: Sumpt. et Typ. Societatis S. Augustini, 1921-1928.

De Palude, Petrus, *Quartus Sententiarum Liber,* Parisiis: Venumdantur a Johanne Petit, 1518.

De Soto, Dominicus, *Liber de Tegendo et Detegendo Secreto,* Salmanticae: Excudebat Joannes Maria a Terranova, 1566.

Diana, Antonius, *Resolutiones Morales,* coordinati per V. P. Martinum de Alcolea, editio novissima, 10 vols., Venetiis: Ex Typographia Balleoniana, 1728.

Doronzo, Emmanuel, *De Poenitentia,* 4 vols., Milwaukee: Bruce Publishing Co., 1949-1953.

Fanfani, Ludovicus, *Manuale Theoretico-Practicum Theologiae Moralis,* 4 vols., Romae: Libraria "Ferrari," 1950-1951.

Ferreres, Joannes B., *Compendium Theologiae Moralis,* editio XVII, X post codicem quam recognovit A. Mondria, 2 vols., Barcinone: E. Subirana, 1949-1950.

Galtier, Paulus, *De Paenitentia,* editio nova, Romae: Pontificia Universitas Gregoriana, 1950.

Genicot, E.-Salsmans, J., *Institutiones Theologiae Moralis,* editio decimaseptima quam paravit A. Gortebecke, 2 vols., Bruxellis: L'Édition Universelle S.A., 1951.

Gury, Joannes, *Compendium Theologiae Moralis,* editio decima, Antonii Ballerini adnotationibus locupletatum, 2 vols., Romae: Ex Typographia S. C. de Propaganda Fide, 1887-1889.

Hürth, F.-Abellan, P. M., *De Sacramentis,* Romae: Pontificia Universitas Gregoriana, 1947.

Iorio, Thomas, *Theologia Moralis,* editio tertia recognita et emendata, 3 vols., Neapoli: M. D'Auria, 1946-1947.

Jone, Heribertus, *Commentarium in Codicem Iuris Canonici,* 3 vols., Paderborn: Officina Libraria Ferdinandi Schöningh, 1950-1955.

Kelly, Gerald, *The Good Confessor,* New York: The Sentinel Press, 1951.

Kurtscheid, Bertrandus, *A History of the Seal of Confession,* tr. by F. A. Marks, St. Louis: B. Herder, 1927.

Lanza, Antonio-Palazzini, Pietro, *Principi di Teologia Morale,* 3 vols., Romae: Editrice Studium, 1952-1956.

Laymann, Paulus, *Theologia Moralis,* Venetiis: Typis Georgii Valentini, 1630.

Lehmkuhl, Augustinus, *Theologia Moralis,* editio decima, 2 vols., Friburgi Brisgoviae: Sumptibus Herder, 1902.

McCarthy, John, *Problems in Theology,* Vol. I, *The Sacraments,* Westminster, Md.: The Newman Press, 1956.

McHugh, John A.-Callan, Charles J., *Moral Theology,* revised and enlarged by Edward P. Farrell, 2 vols., New York: Joseph F. Wagner, 1958.

Merkelbach, Benedictus Henricus, *Quaestiones de Poenitentiae Ministro Eiusque Officiis,* editio altera, aucta et emendata, Liège: La Pensée Catholique, 1935.

———, *Summa Theologiae Moralis,* editio octava aucta et emendata, 3 vols., Montreal: Desclée de Brouwer, 1949.

Murphy, George L., *Delinquencies and Penalties in the Administration and Reception of the Sacraments,* The Catholic University of America Canon Law Studies, n. 17, Washington, D. C.: The Catholic University of America Press, 1923.

Noldin, H.-Schmitt, A., *Summa Theologiae Moralis,* editio XXVII, 3 vols., Barcelona: Editorial Herder, 1951.

Noldin, H.-Schönegger, A., *De Censuris,* editio C. I. C. adaptata XX, Oeniponte: F. Rauch, 1940.

Ojetti, Benedictus, *Synopsis Rerum Moralium et Iuris Pontificii,* editio tertia emandata et aucta, 3 vols., Romae: Ex Officina Polygraphica Editrice, 1909-1912.

Palazzini, P.-De Jorio, A., *Casus Conscientiae,* propositi ac resoluti a pluribus theologis ac canonistis Urbis, 2 vols., Torino: Marietti, 1958.

Piscetta, A.-Gennaro, A., *Elementa Theologiae Moralis,* 7 vols., Vol. V, 6. ed., Torino: Società Editrice Internazionale, 1938.

Pistocchi, Mario, *I Canoni Penali del Codice Ecclesiastico,* Torino: Marietti, 1925.

Prümmer, D. M., *Manuale Theologiae Moralis,* editio decima recognita ab E. M. Münch, 3 vols., Barcelona: Herder, 1945-1946.

Raus, J. B., *Institutiones Canonicae,* altera editio aucta atque emendata, Lugduni: Typis Emmanuelis Vitte, 1931.

Regatillo, Eduardus, *Ius Sacramentarium,* editio secunda, Santander: Sal Terrae, 1949.

Regatillo, E. F.-Zalba, M., *Theologiae Moralis Summa,* 3 vols., Matriti: Biblioteca de Autores Cristianos, 1952-1954.

Reiffenstuel, Anacletus, *Jus Canonicum Universum,* juxta novissimam Romanam editionem R. D. Victoris Pelletier, 7 vols., Parisiis, Apud Ludovicum Vivès, 1864-1870.

———, *Theologia Moralis,* novissime a P. Flaviano Ricci a Cimbria instaurata, 2 vols., Bassani, prostant Venetiis: Apud Remondini, 1773.

Reuter, Joannes, *Neoconfessarius,* ed. Julius Aug. Müllendorff Ratisbonae: Institutum Librarium Pridem G. J. Manz, 1906.

Romani, Sylvius, *Institutiones Juris Canonici,* 2 vols. in 3, Romae: Editrice, "Iustitia," 1941-1945.

———, *Summa Juris Canonici Lineamenta,* Romae: Apud auctorem, 1939.

Rota, Petrus, *Enchiridion Confessarii et Judicis Ecclesiastici,* Augustae Taurinorum: Petrus Marietti, 1884.

Sabetti, Aloysius, *Compendium Theologiae Moralis,* editio XXVII a Timotheo Barrett concinnata, New York: Pustet, 1919.

Salucci, Raffaele, *Il Diritto Penale,* 2 vols., Subiaco: Tipografia dei Monasteri, 1926 1930.

Sanchez, Thomas, *Disputationum de Sancto Matrimonii Sacramento Tomi Tres,* Antverpiae: Apud Henricum Aertssium, 1626.

Savio, Carolus, *Ad Sigillum Sacramentale Animadversiones,* Taurini: Apud F. Casanova et C., 1936.

Schmalzgrueber, Franciscus, *Jus Ecclesiasticum Universum in Quinque Libros Decretalium Gregorii* IX, 5 vols. in 12, Romae: Ex Typographia Rev. Cam. Apostolicae, 1843-1845.

Sipos, Stephanus, *Enchiridion Iuris Canonici,* editionem sextam recognovit Ladislaus Galos, Romae: Orbis Catholicus, 1954.

Suarez, Franciscus, *Opera Omnia,* editio nova, 28 vols. in 30, Parisiis: Apud Ludovicum Vivès, 1856-1878.

Sylvius, Franciscus, *Commentaria in Supplementum sive Additiones ad Tertiam Partem D. Thom. Aquinatis,* Duaci: Sumptibus Marci Wyon, 1622.

Tamburini, Thomas, *Opera Omnia,* 3 vols. in 1, Venetiis: Apud Dominicum Louisam, 1702.

Tanner, Adam, *Theologia Scholastica,* 4 vols., Ingolstadii: Impensis Joannis Bayr, Typis Guilhelmi Ederi, 1626-1627.

Tanquerey, A., *Synopsis Theologiae Moralis et Pastoralis,* 3 vols., Vol. I, editio undecima denuo secundum Codicem recognita, 1930, Tornaci: Desclée et Socii.

Thomas Aquinas, St., *Opera Omnia,* 34 vols., Parisiis: Apud Ludovicum Vivès, 1871-1880.

Vermeersch, A., *Theologia Moralis,* quarta editio a J. Creusen recognita, 3 vols., Romae: Pontificia Universitas Gregoriana, 1948.

Vermeersch, A.-Creusen, J., *Epitome Iuris Canonici,* 3 vols., Vol. II, 6. ed., Romae: H. Dessain, 1940.

Wernz, Franciscus, *Ius Decretalium,* 6 vols., Prati: Ex Officina Libraria Giachetti, 1898-1914.

———, *Ius Canonicum,* ad Codicis normam exactum opera P. Petri Vidal, 7 vols. in 8, Vol. IV, Pars I, 1934; Vol. VII, editio altera recognita, 1951; Romae: Apud Aedes Universitatis Gregorianae.

Wouters, Ludovicus, *Manuale Theologiae Moralis,* 2 vols., Brugis: Carolus Beyaert, 1932-1933.

Woywod, Stanislaus, *A Practical Commentary on the Code of Canon Law,* revised by C. Smith, revised and enlarged edition, 2 vols. in 1, New York: Joseph Wagner, Inc., 1957.

Articles

Allred, Vincent C., "The Confessor in Court," *The Jurist,* XIII (1953), 2-32.

Healy, Edwin, "The Seal of Confession," *Review for Religious,* II (1943), 176-186.

Henriques, C. G. X., "English Law and the Seal of Confession," *Blackfriars,* XIV (1933), 265-272.

Hogan, Edward J., Jr., "The Secrecy of the Confessional and American Courts," *The Catholic Mind,* XLIX (1951), 411-419.

O'Donnell, M. J., "The Seal of Confession," *Irish Ecclesiastical Quarterly,* V (1910), 36-52; VIII (1913), 30-46; 317-333.

PERIODICALS

Blackfriars, Oxford, 1920-
Catholic Mind, The, New York, 1903-
Irish Theological Quarterly, Dublin, 1906-
Jurist, The, Washington, D. C., 1941-
Review for Religious, St. Mary's, Kansas, 1942-

ALPHABETICAL INDEX

BIOGRAPHICAL NOTE

John R. Roos was born in 1930 in Albany, New York. He attended Vincentian Institute of that city; St. Thomas Seminary, Bloomfield, Connecticut; Theological College of The Catholic University of America; and North American College, Rome. Ordained in 1955, he completed his seminary course in 1956, and served for one year as an assistant at the Cathedral of the Immaculate Conception, Albany, before undertaking graduate studies in Canon Law. He received the degree of Master of Arts from The Catholic University of America in 1952; the degree of the Licentiate in Sacred Theology from the Gregorian University in 1956; the degree of the Baccalaureate in Canon Law from The Catholic University of America in 1958; and the degree of the Licentiate in Canon Law from the latter University in 1959.

www.ingramcontent.com/pod-product-compliance
Lightning Source LLC
LaVergne TN
LVHW050207080826
844660LV00012B/372

* 9 7 8 0 8 1 3 2 2 5 7 1 5 *